formatio

**TRADITION. EXPERIENCE.
TRANSFORMATION.**

Formatio books from InterVarsity Press follow the rich tradition of the church in the journey of spiritual formation. These books are not merely about being informed, but about being transformed by Christ and conformed to his image. Formatio stands in InterVarsity Press's evangelical publishing tradition by integrating God's Word with spiritual practice and by prompting readers to move from inward change to outward witness. InterVarsity Press uses the chambered nautilus for Formatio, a symbol of spiritual formation because of its continual spiral journey outward as it moves from its center. We believe that each of us is made with a deep desire to be in God's presence. Formatio books help us to fulfill our deepest desires and to become our true selves in light of God's grace.

Also in English by Joshua Choonmin Kang

Deep-Rooted in Christ: The Way of Transformation

SCRIPTURE BY HEART

Devotional Practices
for Memorizing God's Word

Joshua Choonmin Kang

Foreword by Dallas Willard

IVP Books

An imprint of InterVarsity Press
Downers Grove, Illinois

InterVarsity Press
P.O. Box 1400, Downers Grove, IL 60515-1426
World Wide Web: www.ivpress.com
E-mail: email@ivpress.com

Originally published in 2001 in Korean as Scripture Memorization That Causes Quiet Revolution by Durranna.

InterVarsity Press® is the book-publishing division of InterVarsity Christian Fellowship/USA®, a movement of students and faculty active on campus at hundreds of universities, colleges and schools of nursing in the United States of America, and a member movement of the International Fellowship of Evangelical Students. For information about local and regional activities, write Public Relations Dept., InterVarsity Christian Fellowship/USA, 6400 Schroeder Rd., P.O. Box 7895, Madison, WI 53707-7895, or visit the IVCF website at <www.intervarsity.org>.

All Scripture quotations, unless otherwise indicated, are taken from the New Revised Standard Version of the Bible, copyright 1989 by Division of Christian Education of the National Council of the Churches of Christ in the USA. Used by permission. All rights reserved.

Design: Cindy Kiple

Images: Psalm 23:1-6: Mike Bentley/iStockphoto
        Dove and hills: Kazu Nitta/Getty Images

ISBN 978-0-8308-3536-2

Printed in the United States of America ∞

Library of Congress Cataloging-in-Publication Data

Kang, Joshua Choonmin.
  Scripture by heart: devotional practices for memorizing God's word
  / Joshua Choonmin Kang; foreword by Dallas Willard.
      p. cm.
  Includes bibliographical references and index.
  ISBN 978-0-8308-3536-2 (pbk.: alk. paper)
  1. Bible—Memorizing. I. Title.
  BS617.7.K36 2010
  268'.6—dc22

                                                                    2009035749

P   25 24 23 22 21 20 19 18 17 16 15 14 13 12 11 10 9 8 7 6 5
Y   31 30 29 28 27 26 25 24 23 22 21 20

CONTENTS

Foreword by Dallas Willard 7

Introduction 11

1 Bearing Fruit Through Meditation 17

2 Tasting the Sweetness of the Word 20

   Practice: Take Small Steps 23

3 Understanding the Bible as a Whole 25

4 Forming a Biblical Value System 28

   Practice: Don't Back Out 30

5 Sharpening the Mind 32

6 Acquiring Wisdom 34

   Practice: Sharpen Your Focus 37

7 Dipping into Wisdom 40

8 Cultivating the Affections of Our Heart 43

   Practice: Find the Right Environment 46

9 Overcoming Anxiety 48

10 Enjoying Peace 51

   Practice: Divide and Conquer 53

11 Strengthening the Heart 55

12 Improving the Power of Learning 57

   Practice: Get It Right the First Time 59

13 Developing Concentration 61

14 Strengthening the Will 63

   Practice: Use Index Cards 66

15 Cultivating Ourselves 68

16 Parenting Wisely 70

　　　Practice: *Arrange by Topic* 72

17　Nurturing Disciples 74

18　Maturing as a Teacher 76

　　　Practice: *Make a Habit of It.* 78

19　Dialoguing Well. 81

20　Offering Spiritual Counsel 84

　　　Practice: *Determine Topic, Reference, Word* 87

21　Becoming an Evangelist 88

22　Living in Faith. 91

　　　Practice: *Planning Our Memory Schedule* 93

23　Overcoming Temptation 94

24　Finding Victory in Spiritual Warfare 97

　　　Practice: *Understanding What We Memorize* 100

25　Prevailing Prayer 102

26　Preparing for Spiritual Difficulty. 104

　　　Practice: *Meditation and Transformation* 106

27　Transforming Trials 108

　　　Practice: *Memorize with an Eye on Use* 110

28　Receiving Divine Guidance. 112

　　　Practice: *Memorize for Recollection* 115

29　Becoming God's Instrument 118

　　　Practice: *Aim for Mastery.* 121

30　Fulfilling Your Mission 125

　　　Practice: *When Memorization Bogs Down* 127

Conclusion: Meditating on Psalm 1 141

Appendix: Favorite Passages for Memorization 152

FOREWORD

The apostle Paul tells us to present our bodies to God in such a way that we will be transformed by the renewing of our minds (Romans 12:1-2). Most who read him today stop right there, thinking perhaps, *What good advice!* But they do not proceed to implement it. They do not take it seriously as a doorway into the blessed life with Christ in his kingdom. They do not welcome it as a reality that will carry them away from conformity to a social existence—even a religious one—that is actually in defiance of God, and plant them solidly in the eternal kingdom that is here now.

In part this is because they do not understand the mind and do not know how to move toward its renewal. They are apt to become passive and not understand *their* part in the divine work of "mind transplant."

The human mind is filled with feelings, ideas, images, ways of reasoning, habits of thought, memories and expectations of various kinds. Many of these are enslaving, harmful and false. They shape our actual beliefs and guide our actions. No doubt we most go wrong in *how we think* about God and about our life before God. It is in this area more than anywhere else that our minds must be renewed for the sake of the transformation of our whole life into godliness.

God will help us, but our part is also indispensable. What are we to do? The simplest and most effective way of mind renewal in Christ is memorization of Scripture: large passages of it as well as individual verses. That is why memorization must play such a large part in spiritual transformation. The human mind is quite small and limited in terms of what can consciously occupy it, but we have some choice as to what is present there. We must choose well.

Memorization of Scripture is one way of "taking charge" of the contents of our conscious thoughts, and of the feelings, beliefs and actions that depend on them. Ancient followers of God understood this well:

> Thy word have I hid in mine heart,
>   that I might not sin against thee. (Psalm 119:11 KJV)

> Thy word is a lamp unto my feet,
>   and a light unto my path. (Psalm 119:105 KJV)

> The entrance of thy words giveth light. (Psalm 119:130 KJV)

Our life takes a godly and good direction when our mind is consciously occupied with God's written words. Those words then increasingly eliminate the conscious mental contents that would surely lead us away from God.

But when we take the Scriptures in by memorization, the words of God also affect our lives far beyond our consciousness. We come to live "by every word that proceeds from the mouth of God" (Matthew 4:4 RSV). Through memorization God's words reside in our body, in our social environment, in the constant orientation of our will and in the depths of our soul. They become a power, a substance, that sustains and directs us without our even thinking of them, and they emerge into conscious thought and action as needed. This is what Jesus spoke of as *abiding, dwelling in him:* "If you abide in me, and my words abide in you, ask whatever you will, and it shall be done for you. By this my Father is glorified, that you bear much fruit, and so prove to be my disciples" (John 15:7-8 RSV).

Joshua Choonmin Kang helps us to appreciate and appropriate the power for transformation into Christlikeness that comes from knowing the Scriptures "by heart." He gives us encouraging words about the many good effects of memorization, and excellent instruction on how to go about memorizing the Scriptures. If you will absorb his teachings and do what he says—adapting it to your personal circumstances and making it a persistent part of your day-to-day life—then you will experience the renewal of your mind and undergo the transformation of life which everyone knows should come from following Jesus closely. Grace will see to it. The Word of God which is "living and powerful" (Hebrews 4:12 NKJV) will form you in the likeness of Christ.

Dallas Willard

INTRODUCTION

My workshop topic for the Renovaré International Conference in Denver was Scripture memorization. Since I was unknown to most of the attendees and would be speaking in Korean, which would be translated into English, I thought few would attend. But when the doors were closed, there were close to fifty people in the room.

The first ten minutes went well, but then people, perhaps as many as a dozen, began slipping from the room. I thought it was the multilingual presentation or even the perennial difficulty of the topic. The real reason, I later discovered, is that they were looking for a 101 quick-tips-and-tricks-to-memorizing presentation—ideas that could apply to memorizing anything from Scripture to phone numbers to facts and figures.

When I asked the remaining crowd if they found me difficult to understand, they said no. They even asked me to continue in English. Then in halting phrases I spent the next forty minutes presenting my plan.

My main message: to memorize the Bible, we have to pray the Bible first. Nothing easy, nothing quick about it. Those who stayed in the workshop seemed genuinely moved.

WHY MEMORIZE THE BIBLE?

I can think of four reasons.

To know God. All we need to know about God, at least on earth, the Bible tells us. It records God's life and his works. It quotes Jesus as saying that in eternal life we will know more about God. But for now the Bible is our best source for learning about God.

The whole world should be filled with the knowledge of God.

> They will not hurt or destroy
> > on all my holy mountain;
> for the earth will be full of the knowledge of the LORD
> > as the waters cover the sea. (Isaiah 11:9)

Hosea echoes the same note.

> I desire steadfast love and not sacrifice,
> > the knowledge of God rather than burnt-offerings.
> (Hosea 6:6)

David strikes a similar chord.

> Taste and see that the LORD is good;
> > happy are those who take refuge in him. (Psalm 34:8)

It's one thing to know about God the way we know any fact, but it's quite another thing to meet God. To meet God is to love him. But how can we love him if we can't see him face to face? How can we love a person we don't know?

To imitate Christ. Everyone in the New Testament who personally received Christ was called a *disciple,* and with that came a responsibility. Disciples must emulate their teacher. They must imitate the teacher's way of thinking and acting. As the disciples do this, they become more like Christ himself. But it doesn't happen overnight; it's a gradual, never-ending process.

Beyond believing in the Lord, a true disciple will come to know him. Beyond knowing him, each disciple will come to love him. Paul says as much to the Ephesians. In loving him we mature "to the measure of the full stature of Christ" (Ephesians 4:13).

Disciples of Christ have to go to school. They have to become apprentices studying under the divine Master and learning Christ's key teachings as recorded in the Bible. Living in a later century we too, if we want to become disciples of the same Lord, have to go to the same school. We have to memorize the same passages. We have to learn them heart and soul before we can teach them to others.

When we commit the Word to memory and abide in it, we receive spiritual insight. Only when we see straight and deep do we bear fruit. We have this on the authority of Jesus himself: "As for what was sown on good soil, this is the one who hears the word and understands it, who indeed bears fruit and yields, in one case a hundredfold, in another sixty, and in another thirty" (Matthew 13:23).

The varieties of fruit Jesus speaks of here, character and ministry, are found in the divine orchard; that is to say, in Christ's own life. Hence, to bear the fruit of imitating Christ, we must get Christ's words down to a T.

To worship God. Worshiping God is the cause of our existence, the very reason for our existence. The Lord puts it quite plainly. "My chosen people [are] / the people whom I formed for myself / so that they might declare my praise" (Isaiah 43:20-21).

Whatever we do in everyday life is related to worship. Certainly God honors those who are committed workers for his kingdom. But before we commit ourselves to such work, we must become true worshipers. Mary of Bethany is a good example; she was a true worshiper at the feet of Jesus before she used her precious jar of perfume on him. Even today the power of committed service has its source in true worship. Mary pleased the Lord with her worshipful act, and we please the Lord with similar acts of worship.

God seeks true worshipers. Jesus made this explicit when he spoke to the woman at the well.

The hour is coming, and is now here, when the true worshippers will worship the Father in spirit and truth, for the Father seeks such as these to worship him. God is spirit, and those who worship him must worship in spirit and truth. (John 4:23-24)

Worshiping "in Spirit" means worshiping in the Holy Spirit; worshiping "in truth" means according to the truth, that is, according to the Word of God. Aaron's sons are an illustration of those who do just the opposite.

Aaron's sons, Nadab and Abihu, each took his censer, put fire in it, and laid incense on it; and they offered unholy fire before the LORD, such as he had not commanded them. And fire came out from the presence of the LORD and consumed them, and they died before the LORD. (Leviticus 10:1-2)

We have been called to worship him according to the Scriptures.

To fulfill God's mission. Jesus committed the Scriptures to memory and had full mastery over them. His being was filled with the Scriptures. As a child he grew in wisdom on account of them. He walked in them, proclaimed them even from the cross, even as he was accomplishing God's work of redemption.

Jesus commissioned his first disciples to make disciples of their own, and not only in Judea but in all the nations of the world (Matthew 28:19-20). To fulfill this mission the disciples had to learn the words of Christ by heart. Once the Scriptures were impressed on their hearts, they were ready to teach everything that the Lord had commanded.

The disciples weren't able to carry the Scriptures in book form as we do today. They had to depend on their memory to fulfill their mission. If the Scriptures had not been memorized, they would never have been recorded on paper.

In the footsteps of the first disciples, we too have a mission to the world. We must diligently commit the books of the Bible to memory, which will transform our hearts as stewards prepared with the truth of his Word.

The apostle Paul speaks to this point explicitly: "Do your best to present yourself to God as one approved by him, a worker who has no need to be ashamed, rightly explaining the word of truth" (2 Timothy 2:15).

GETTING THE MOST OUT OF THIS BOOK

After this book was published in Korean, I had it rendered into readable English. It contains thirty meditations on memorizing the Bible, each reflecting one of the many spiritual benefits of memorization. The chapters begin with a Scripture verse taken from the chapter. You may want to commit these key verses to memory as you read along.

Interwoven with the chapters are seventeen practices that will help you learn to memorize. I was formed in the practice of Scripture memory in part by the Navigators' very fine workbook and set of Scripture memory cards: *Topical Memory System*. Some of the practices in these pages reflect practices I first learned in those pages.

As a conclusion to the book to illustrate the fruitfulness of instant Bible recall, I've included a personal meditation of my own. In the appendix you will find one hundred of my favorite verses for memorization, organized topically. Allow God to lead you to the verses from these pages that you need to commit to heart for encouragement and spiritual growth.

When should we read, pray, memorize? Every day without exception. No less than fifteen minutes and no more than thirty minutes a day. One chapter a week should be manageable by most readers. If you find yourself overwhelmed, turn to the final practice, "When Memorization Bogs Down," for a week's refreshment and ideas for getting unstuck. Then return to the spot where you left off.

What should you do when you finish this book? Begin again! Continue in this way until the booster rocket falls away and is no longer needed.

NEW MODE OF PRAYER

Those of you who are already familiar with prayer in its many forms may see *Scripture by Heart* as a sort of *lectio divina*, pausing at an agree-

able text, mulling it over, meditating on it until the Lord begins to
speak to you and you speak back to the Lord.

And so *Scripture by Heart* is a sort of memorization divina, a collec-
tion of my most treasured retrievable quotations from the book of
books!

Even if memorization isn't one of the goals of your spiritual life,
you'll find much to rummage through in this book, material well
worth meditating on. However you use this humble book, the Lord
will surely bless your effort.

1

BEARING FRUIT
THROUGH MEDITATION

As for that in the good soil, these are the ones who,
when they hear the word, hold it fast in an honest and good heart,
and bear fruit with patient endurance.

LUKE 8:15

Learning Scripture by heart throws open the door to meditation. When we meditate deeply on the words of Scripture, we begin to bear fruit. But before we can meditate scripturally, we must have a scriptural treasury in our heart. The words of Scripture must be safely deposited in the vaults and chambers of our innermost heart.

Scripture meditation is like a cow chewing her cud. Naturally, feeding upon the Word of God comes first; we must "take in" the words of Scripture. Then, just as the cow brings up her food for renewed grinding, we chew on biblical thoughts deliberately and thoroughly; that is to say, we digest the words, mulling them over in our minds and hearts.

It must be remembered that digesting the Word is more important than ingesting it; food itself is of no use to us until it's converted into energy. Digested food supplies the needs of the body through blood, and thus may be said to provide life itself. Memorizing the Word is like ingesting food, while meditating is digesting the food.

Jesus compares the Word of God to a seed (Luke 8:11). Seeds are small and hard to handle, but each is full of life. One seed contains thousands of apple trees. One fig contains a thousand seeds. As someone has wisely said, the mystery of life is contained in a seed.

Each word of Scripture is a seed. Plant each word in your interior garden and you will bear more fruit than your limbs can support. We can assess the spiritual richness of people by the lushness of their spiritual gardens, which will flourish as they memorize Scripture.

A shepherd who feeds a flock with the words of God has enriched them beyond expectation. But the shepherd will remain poor until he or she is filled with the same rich fodder. The more Scripture the shepherd memorizes, the healthier the flock becomes and the quicker it multiplies.

A farmer reaps what is sown and no more. If the farmer has sown in good ground, the crop will burst out all over. This seems to be a law of farming and may well be a law of spirituality; men and women of God will eventually reap more spiritual fruit than they know what to do with.

A farmer plants the seeds, nurtures the plants and harvests the fruit. In this sense, meditation is like the period between planting the seed and bearing the fruit, or the period between the ingestion and the digestion.

The first letter of Peter has a similar progression. First it urges its readers to rid themselves of malice, guile, insincerity, envy, slander. Then, "like newborn infants, long for the pure, spiritual milk, so that by it you may grow into salvation" (1 Peter 2:2).

Peter's advice remains current for today's Christians. When we meditate on the Word of God, we will memorize the Word of God. And when we memorize the Word of God, our spiritual life will flourish like never before.

2

TASTING THE SWEETNESS
OF THE WORD

How sweet are your words to my taste,

sweeter than honey to my mouth!

PSALM 119:103

Memorizing is hard at first but grows easier with time. Those who persevere will experience an odd sensation. King David did: "With open mouth I pant, / because I long for your commandments" (Psalm 119:131). Apparently, his longing had become habitual.

We have all seen an infant's mouth eagerly longing for its mother's milk, or a baby bird screeching for its mother's food. The memory of a delicious dinner is enough to excite a ravenous appetite.

A person who has tasted the Word just once will have a lifelong craving. David developed a sweet tooth, as Psalm 119 reveals. "How sweet are your words to my taste, / sweeter than honey to my mouth!" (v. 103).

The fear of the Lord is pure,
    enduring forever;

the ordinances of the Lord are true
    and righteous altogether.
More to be desired are they than gold,
    even much fine gold;
sweeter also than honey,
    and drippings of the honeycomb. (Psalm 19:9-10)

This has been my experience as well, but at the beginning it wasn't so. Trying to memorize the Word was hard. If I experienced any taste at all, it was one of bitterness. Pressing on, however, I began to sense the sweetness of the Word. A whole new world of truth opened up. I experienced a kind of joy and blessed happiness previously unknown to me.

A sense of dullness in my spiritual life began to dissipate. A sense of awareness took its place. I found myself meditating on God's Word or listening to recorded sermons. I couldn't get enough of God's words in whatever form. Before I knew it, I was rejoicing with David in one of his honeyed psalms. "The unfolding of your words gives light; / it imparts understanding to the simple" (Psalm 119:130).

Enjoying the Word this way may be an acquired taste. Some prefer soup simmered for hours in a crockpot; others are satisfied with instant soup mix blistered in a saucepan or blasted by a microwave. I prefer the pot; it reminds me of the grace we receive when we meditate on the words of God, mulling over them, stirring the pot slowly, as though they were the centerpiece of a spiritual feast. Apparently King David has stirred the same pot. "O taste and see that the LORD is good; / happy are those who take refuge in him" (Psalm 34:8).

When Scripture memory has become habitual, we hear the preaching of the Word more clearly. It increases our knowledge; it stimulates our interest; it develops our thirst for deeper understanding. The person who sits next to us who can't remember a Scripture verse to save his life hears quite a different sermon.

Occasionally, we are deeply touched by a Scripture reference in a sermon. We've heard it before and perhaps have drawn a conclusion or two about its contents. But in the light of certain other Scripture verses already memorized, the passage leaps to life.

Of course we have the Holy Spirit to thank for that. He brings conviction to our hearts by applying the meaning of the text to our own particular situation.

My prayer is that we would find joy in savoring these benefits, lingering over the Scriptures as we commit them to memory.

PRACTICE

Take Small Steps

We begin memorizing Scripture by taking small steps, then expanding gradually to larger steps. Be patient with yourself, especially whenever you're tempted to memorize Leviticus in an hour and a half!

Three key Bible passages will help us maintain our pace, however humble it may be.

> He put before them another parable: "The kingdom of heaven is like a mustard seed that someone took and sowed in his field; it is the smallest of all the seeds, but when it has grown it is the greatest of shrubs and becomes a tree, so that the birds of the air come and make nests in its branches." (Matthew 13:31-32)

> Though your beginning was small,
>   your latter days will be very great. (Job 8:7)

> The least of them shall become a clan,
>   and the smallest one a mighty nation;
> I am the Lord;
>   in its time I will accomplish it quickly. (Isaiah 60:22)

Start, start, start! Whether willingly or unwillingly, we all start small. The old saying "Little drops of water make the mighty ocean" is certainly true. But still it's hard to take the first step. Postponing won't help; it will only make things harder.

As hard as the first step is, the second step is often harder. A bold initiative is required. "You can't get second things by putting them first," C. S. Lewis once remarked in an essay; "you can get second things only by putting first things first" ("First and Second Things" in *God in the Dock*).

Emotion follows motion. Starting is half the work. Even if you don't feel like it, put it into motion and emotion will be sure to follow. Once you begin memorizing the Word, you'll be literally affected by the Word.

If you understand the value, benefit and heart's proper attitude of memorizing Scripture, you're ready to take the first step.

Climbing a mountain, running a marathon, walking a continent—they all begin with the first step. Similarly, with the Bible it begins with a single verse and proceeds with one verse at a time.

Walt Kallestad, a pastor and popular author, offers this encouraging remark in his book *Wake Up Your Dreams:* "The greatest challenge for the great vision is taking the first step. Yes, indeed. Begin resolutely. Jump in boldly!"

3

UNDERSTANDING THE BIBLE AS A WHOLE

Long ago God spoke to our ancestors
in many and various ways by the prophets,
but in these last days he has spoken to us by a Son,
whom he appointed heir of all things,
through whom he also created the worlds.

HEBREWS 1:1-2

Every child of God should know the Bible well. But those who minister to others should know the Bible inside out. If they don't, they're fooling nobody but themselves.

We can be said to know the Bible when we can range from one end of Scripture to the other, discovering common threads and themes, weighing different interpretations, paying more attention to some passages than to others. When we undertake a sizable program of Scripture memory, we soon begin to connect the dots and a central theme may emerge like a string of pearls.

One such example is Stephen's sermon recorded in the seventh chapter of the Acts of the Apostles. He was a layperson who possessed a rabbi's mastery of Scripture. When it came to defending himself against capital charges, he was able to recall key passages and major themes of the Old Testament. He could recount biblical history in the light of the person of Christ. In answering troublesome issues raised by intellectuals, Stephen turned the tables on them. John recorded Jesus saying to the Jews, "You search the scriptures because you think that in them you have eternal life; and it is they that testify on my behalf" (John 5:39).

According to the apostle Paul, anyone who masters the Bible perceives Christ in every passage. "We destroy arguments and every proud obstacle raised up against the knowledge of God, and we take every thought captive to obey Christ" (2 Corinthians 10:4-5).

In the same vein, a thorough knowledge of the Bible entails understanding the mysteries of God. According to Paul, the overall mystery is none other than Jesus Christ. "To [the saints] God chose to make known how great among the Gentiles are the riches of the glory of this mystery, which is Christ in you, the hope of glory" (Colossians 1:27).

Another mystery is the gospel. Paul says, "Pray also for me, so that when I speak, a message may be given to me to make known with boldness the mystery of the gospel" (Ephesians 6:19).

Still another mystery is the kingdom of God and the church: " 'A man will leave his father and mother and be joined to his wife, and the two will become one flesh.' This is a great mystery, and I am applying it to Christ and the church" (Ephesians 5:31-32).

According to the Gospel of Matthew, the divine reality was more than a human mind could contain; that's why Jesus used parables when he wanted to teach the kingdom. "Jesus told the crowds all these things in parables; without a parable he told them nothing. This was to fulfill what had been spoken through the prophet" (Matthew 13:34-35).

A comprehensive knowledge also recognizes the progressive nature of scriptural revelation—how the Old Testament contains much of New Testament teaching. According to the author of Hebrews, "Long ago God spoke to our ancestors in many and various ways by the prophets, but in these last days he has spoken to us by a Son, whom he appointed heir of all things, through whom he also created the worlds" (Hebrews 1:1-2).

Quite obviously, Jesus, our model in so many other ways, is also a model in this one. He mastered Scripture, knew the verses by heart and interpreted the Old Testament in light of the history of redemption.

It's never too early, and never too late, to begin a serious program of Scripture memory with a view to mastering the meaning of the Bible as a whole. Just know that you're not alone in the process. The Spirit plays his part, anointing our spirit, offering us the grace of his teaching.

4

FORMING A BIBLICAL VALUE SYSTEM

Train children in the right way,
and when old, they will not stray.

PROVERBS 22:6

Values reveal the character of a person. They identify our treasures, our loves. But when asked what our values are, we often feel embarrassed, hem and haw, mumble something that may be just the opposite of what they truly are.

To discover our own values, all we have to do is ask a series of questions. What delighted us last week? What did we think about? What did we do? Who did we spend time with? What did we spend our money on?

When it comes to value formation in children, educational psychologists tell us, the earlier, the better. The first five years are critical. But if we do nothing in this regard, the world will take over and ruin our children. Happily, if we parents do our duty right from the start, we give our children the most precious gift.

Parents must be examples first, transferring values by modeling. When we learn Scripture by heart, cherishing and delighting in the process, our children will quickly follow. Soon they too learn to honor the One who has given us Scripture.

For the rest of their lives Scripture will be a blessing to them and others.

The Jews have always taught their children to love the God of Scripture. This bit of practical wisdom has been enshrined in the Old Testament. "Train children in the right way, / and when old, they will not stray" (Proverbs 22:6).

As kingdom builders, we live in two worlds, the visible and the invisible. But we place a greater value on the invisible, the eternal Word and human souls. Scripture memorization helps us examine the true focus of our hearts and enables us to see our true selves.

We can't live on this earth forever. While here, we exist only to fulfill God's purpose, only to glorify him. Scripture helps, putting greater value on the heavenly than the earthly, the eternal rather than the temporal, the invisible rather than the visible.

Certainly there's a need for balance when living out the Scripture-filled life. We must always seek the spiritual in the mundane, but we shouldn't despise the principles of accomplishing a task successfully. Yet, all these are the means we use to fulfill the will of God.

My prayer is that we begin this process by learning Scripture by heart. Forget the glimmer and the glamour of the world. Just pray the text at hand.

PRACTICE

Don't Back Out

The freedom to choose is one of God's great gifts to humankind. As a result our lives abound in choices and resolutions. Choices create energy. At the beginning, if we really mean what we choose, creative ideas come to mind and circumstances fall into place. Specific means to achieve the goal are developed. But more than anything else, our initial resolve has to be ironclad.

Interest rather than ability. Many people think they don't have a good memory, but this isn't quite true. Many people simply aren't interested in memorizing anything. That said, we certainly remember special days, telephone numbers and addresses, and we don't forget our friends' names. We also remember the birthdays of those we love. The same is true of memorizing Scripture. While many have a mild interest in doing so, a few actually resolve to do it, no matter what the obstacles.

Conscious effort. When we are convinced of the necessity and consciously exert major effort, we can remember just about anything. We rehearse what we want to remember, and we reflect on what we've memorized. Scripture memorization succeeds only to the degree we want it to. Most are content to doodle and dawdle around in short-term memory. A few, however, are determined to deposit their memorized verses into long-term memory, and these succeed.

Turning back is not an option. Whenever I'm tempted to stop memorizing the Word, I reflect on a text in Hebrews. "'My righteous one will live by faith. My soul takes no pleasure in anyone who shrinks back.' But we are not among those who shrink back and so are lost, but among those who have faith and so are saved" (Hebrews 10:38-39).

In memorizing the Word I remind myself that I'm walking by faith and that although I know I can, I won't turn back.

5

SHARPENING THE MIND

*Solid food is for the mature, for those whose faculties
have been trained by practice to distinguish good from evil.*

HEBREWS 5:14

A healthy spirituality sends deep roots into a cultivated mind; knowledge is essential to spiritual development. We feel and act upon knowledge because our thoughts affect our feelings. The mind also influences the will because our choices depend on our knowledge.

Yes, the mind narrowcasts, but, including as it does intuitive and experiential knowing, it also broadcasts to our whole being. It widens our horizon and deepens our perspective, it embraces life, and it truly cultivates the mind.

When I refer to the mind, therefore, I mean more than mere possession of knowledge. It includes a variety of powers. Consciousness. Vigilance. Concentration. Perception. Spiritual sensitivity. An excellent mind can see through the "window" of the soul.

Developing spiritual sensitivity is a rigorous exercise; but it's no more rigorous than growing and maturing general perceptivity.

Learning Scripture by heart develops perception in both mind and soul. Maturity very often depends on this perceptive capacity.

The letter to the Hebrews says much the same thing. "Solid food is for the mature, for those whose faculties have been trained by practice to distinguish good from evil" (Hebrews 5:14). An immature person, on the other hand, can't tell bad from good.

Cultivation of the mind requires habitual training of the thought processes. We often say that we want to "sharpen up our minds" or "hone" our arguments. One way to achieve this is to learn Scripture by heart. Impressing words onto our hearts is no easy job, but the reward is significant. As our perceiving skills are developed, our mind increases in sensitivity so that all things are seen in new light and in greater depth.

To change the world we must first change the way we see it; we must see it from a different perspective. A cultivated mind can see the universe in a falling leaf, an orchard in a seed, an ocean in a drop of water, eternity in a grain of sand.

A cultivated mind produces more insight, possesses a richer sense of the world and enjoys a more attractive experience of reality. Our minds are influenced by what comes from outside of us. We cannot create our own world, and yet we can create our own worldview. The abundance and vitality of the world we live in depends on how we see it. When our minds are cultivated by the Word of God through Scripture memorization, we can see the world that was created by God in the way that God sees it.

In this respect, learning Scripture by heart expands our imagination while at the same time sharpening our capacity to think.

6

Acquiring Wisdom

She is more precious than jewels,
and nothing you desire can compare with her.

PROVERBS 3:15

One of the most enjoyable spiritual pastimes is drawing a Scripture verse from memory and meditating on it. Often meditation is a joy of its own, but gaining wisdom while doing so leads to ecstasy.

The world is a circus of sin—temporary pleasures surround us and abound in us. Worldly wisdoms may produce a joy that is pale and wan when compared to the extreme joy we experience when we find eternal wisdom. The book of Proverbs has nailed this sentiment. "Doing wrong is like sport to a fool, / but wise conduct is pleasure to a person of understanding" (Proverbs 10:23).

To lead a life in search of wisdom we must learn Scripture by heart. Scripture contains half a dozen major treasuries of practical and spiritual wisdom. When we store them up in our heart, we deepen out reservoir of wisdom. When we meditate, we lower our ladle into the clear, cool water and refresh our spirit to hitherto unknown heights.

Wisdom is a most precious commodity in our spiritual life:

> She [Wisdom] is more precious than jewels,
> and nothing you desire can compare with her.
> Long life is in her right hand;
> in her left hand are riches and honor.
> Her ways are ways of pleasantness,
> and all her paths are peace. (Proverbs 3:15-17)

Wisdom builds better houses and better warriors:

> By wisdom a house is built,
> and by understanding it is established;
> by knowledge the rooms are filled
> with all precious and pleasant riches.
> Wise warriors are mightier than strong ones. (Proverbs 24:3-5)

Luke, who gave us the infancy narrative, underscores the value of wisdom: "Jesus increased in wisdom and in years, and in divine and human favor" (Luke 2:52). Paul says much the same thing: "In [Jesus] are hidden all the treasures of wisdom and knowledge" (Colossians 2:3).

Paul exhorts the Corinthians to mature in wisdom: "Brothers and sisters, do not be children in your thinking; rather, be infants in evil, but in thinking be adults" (1 Corinthians 14:20).

Spiritual wisdom differs from worldly wile. The former is virtuous and vertical, while the latter is only lazy and horizontal. Wisdom comes from God above, whereas cunning issues from the devil. Wisdom is spiritual, but the latter is material. If wisdom is telescopic, shrewdness is microscopic. The core of wisdom lies in the power of discernment. It discerns good and evil when found in time, place, position, language and people. It comes from above.

Wisdom is the principle that isolates the idea that overcomes a crisis at hand. It's the reflex that turns a crisis into an opportunity. With a long-standing track record of learning Scripture by heart and sharpening the art of meditating on them, we can respond wisely in all situations, discerning, choosing, acting decisively.

The secret to Joshua's victory lay in wisdom. "Joshua son of Nun was full of the spirit of wisdom, because Moses had laid his hands on him; and the Israelites obeyed him, doing as the LORD had commanded Moses" (Deuteronomy 34:9).

PRACTICE

Sharpen Your Focus

Concentration is necessary to bring any action to a satisfactory conclusion. As light passes through a magnifying glass and focuses on an object, the light is multiplied many times, creating incredible energy.

Sharpen the focus. Successful memorizing of the Word requires sharpening our ability to focus. When we're interested, we naturally focus and shut the rest of the world out. When we're not that interested, we put the magnifying glass down and pick up something else; we become preoccupied. But when we're really interested, we don't mind spending the time.

Memorizing the Word is one of the lofty delights of life. Alas, too few people today have discovered this. But the psalmist knew it millennia ago. "Their delight is in the law of the LORD, / and on his law they meditate day and night" (Psalm 1:2).

Set a goal. We can't focus if we have nothing to focus on. We need to decide which book of the Bible we'll memorize first, then how many verses we'll memorize by the end of the week, the month, the year. The focus becomes a promise, and before we've memorized a verse, we'll experience the delicate taste of victory.

Set a deadline. Nothing develops a focus so much as a deadline. Lexicographer and literary critic Samuel Johnson once quipped, "Anyone sentenced to the gallows in fifteen days will develop a wonderful power to remember." In our own time the day before vacation is a wildly productive one.

When we don't have a deadline, our concentration diminishes, wanders off, takes a nap; we have to drag ourselves to do the simplest task.

According to Parkinson's Law, whimsically promulgated by British economist C. Northcote Parkinson, "Work expands to fill the time allotted." "Work will progress only as much as the assigned amount of time." I'm more interested in a corollary of that law, "assign less time for each task, and you will get it done much faster."

I've discovered that the closer I am to the deadline in preparing a sermon or writing a book, the greater the creative energy I have. Naturally, I give myself an earlier deadline than need be as insurance that I'll actually meet the real deadline. If I don't do this, I stress out, and the quality of my work in progress drops off.

Educate your mind. An intimate relationship can be observed between concentration and other different kinds of thinking. Jung Jae Chun, director of Light and Love Reading Clinic in Pasadena, California, stresses the good effects of tough, intensive training in the areas of cognition, memory, convergent and divergent thinking, evaluation, and analytical and critical thinking.

As a rule we don't excel in concentration; our minds tend to wander, or they stay fixed on a one-track activity for a long time. Alas, there is an intimate correlation between concentration and thinking. It's just that we don't think much about anything. No wonder we're not able to concentrate well.

Although thinking isn't an easy activity, it is possible to train our minds to think more and better. Rich dividends await the trained mind. To some, it seems like diving into ocean depths and discovering a wealth of treasures.

Tickle your curiosity. We should educate our children to think from early on. We should see that they have access to books and games and puzzles, and access to drawing materials. We should encourage them to think there's no such thing as a bad question.

"I myself have no special talent," Albert Einstein once said; "curiosity, obsession, and dogged endurance, combined with self-criticism, have brought me to my ideas" (as cited in *Preaching That Connects* by Mark Galli and Craig Brian Larson).

Curiosity is a ticklish form of knowing, providing a continuous stream of material to be analyzed by each person.

As Michael J. Gelb, a leading authority on the application of genius thinking to personal and organizational development, rightly says in *How to Think Like Leonardo da Vinci*, "Curiosity is a desire to know, a desire to learn, a passion to grow, a generator for knowledge and wisdom."

Your power to concentrate will increase as you continue to memorize Scripture verses and apply these principles.

7

DIPPING INTO WISDOM

Keep these words that I am
commanding you today in your heart.

DEUTERONOMY 6:6

If there is a common ground between saints of the past and of the present, both of whom led lives of blessing and beauty, it is this: they explored the inner world of the mind and wisely exploited what they found there. By doing so these faithful servants of God acquired a keen insight into the mind of the Godhead as well as that of humankind.

God poured his mind into the Word so that we might receive it in written form. We pour our mind over Scripture so that we might learn the mind of God. According to the Deuteronomist we learn the mind of God by learning Scripture by heart.

Keep these words that I am commanding you today in your heart. Recite them to your children and talk about them when you are at home and when you are away, when you lie down and when you rise. Bind them as a sign on your hand, fix them as an emblem on your forehead, and write them on the doorposts of your house and on your gates. (Deuteronomy 6:6-9)

Here we must give special heed to the words *in your heart;* this is the beginning of our union with the mind of God. As we read his words we learn his intentions, his concerns and his ultimate purpose.

Keeping God's concerns in our heart is reason enough for impressing his words on our minds. Proverbs puts it strongly. "Keep your heart with all vigilance, / for from it flow the springs of life" (Proverbs 4:23); that means God has established a watershed in our heart. In fact, he perceives the condition of our heart as he blesses us and works through us.

Our mind contains our plans and purposes; it's something like a well of wisdom. Again Proverbs has the last best word: "The purposes in the human mind are like deep water, / but the intelligent will draw them out" (Proverbs 20:5).

The strongest person knows his or her inner thoughts and rules over them. "One who is slow to anger is better than the mighty, / and one whose temper is controlled [is mightier] than one who captures a city" (Proverbs 16:32).

In search of excellence throughout history, many have studied the conscious, subconscious and superconscious minds. They've also plumbed unconscious thoughts or so-called potential subconscious. The subconscious is hidden deeply in our inner mind; the superconscious comes down from above. For Christians, the superconscious is the mind filled with the Holy Spirit.

Entry into the world of mystery is solitude. We do so by means of meditating on Scripture and waiting silently. We forsake all distractions of the mind through repentance and focus on short verses of Scripture. This allows us to hear the still, small voice of God, which is made aware by the profound and incomparable words of wisdom. Inspiring and profound wisdom is the grace given to those who thirst for this unrivaled time of fellowship with him.

The world of our inner being is indeed full of mystery. The moment we receive Jesus as our Lord, according to Paul, the wisdom of God comes our way (Colossians 2:3). At the same time, the Spirit of wisdom takes residence in us (Isaiah 11:2). In the same way, believers can also experience the coming of this wisdom as we learn Scripture by heart.

Our mind, moreover, becomes like a well of wisdom. Constant use widens the underground channels through which the water supply flows. Our mind overflows with wisdom only with regular and diligent learning and meditation.

Previously cultivated channels of wisdom and newly learned verses of Scripture meet to bring forth still more insight. And this insight deepens when we engage in further meditation of the Word.

The deep calls the deep. The secret of the well is that the more you use it, the more abundant the well becomes. If you don't pump out the water, the well dries up. So people operate the pump even when they don't need water for use. They use the pump and draw the water out in order to keep the well from drying up. The well dries up not because we use it too much, but because we don't use it.

My prayer is that you'll draw wisdom in abundance through meditating on the Word and making sense out of its meaning.

8

Cultivating the Affections of Our Heart

Keep your heart with all vigilance,
for from it flow the springs of life.

PROVERBS 4:23

Learning Scriptures will cultivate not only our perceptivity but also our affectivity.

Knowing how to express our emotion positively is a key to building healthy social relationships.

Developing a well-balanced affectivity (emotional life) is like tending and cultivating an interior garden.

Memorizing Scripture is like planting seeds in the garden of our heart. Again the Deuteronomist: "keep these words that I am commanding you today in your heart" (Deuteronomy 6:6).

By constant cultivation you become well aware of the interior of your being, so that the affections of the heart can also be attended.

In his book *Emotional Intelligence*, Daniel Goleman, professor of psychology at Harvard, claims that emotional quotient (EQ) is a more powerful indicator of success in life than intelligence quotient (IQ). He surveyed prominent figures throughout history and discovered that most of them weren't endowed with high IQ but rather with high EQ. The list of traits he identifies include self-control, compassion, love, patience, diligence, compromise, honesty, creativity; all of these may be found in the interior garden.

Goleman intimates that there may be a closer relation between success and perceptions of affectivity/emotionality than to intelligence. How can this be? The world of understanding and perception is a sanctified world of the senses in which disparate parts sometimes find connection, instantly producing a comprehensive understanding. This intuitive insight defies logic, but it can be experienced by persons who generally have a well-ordered interior life.

Insight may be described as an experience during the sober and quiet moments when all of the factors under consideration come into full view with immediacy. It is as if the whole universe is reflected in a clear mind. Indeed, it's a gift from God for those who will set aside times for reflection and meditation on his Word.

This isn't an experience for special groups of elites; rather it awaits anyone who genuinely longs to gain insight and understanding. The psalmist knew who these experiences were for. "He satisfies the thirsty, / and the hungry he fills with good things" (Psalm 107:9).

A person with a high EQ will have a well-ordered interior life. He or she already possesses wisdom to utilize the heart, which is the wellspring of life. The Wisdom Literature taught this some millennia ago. "Keep your heart with all vigilance, / for from it flow the springs of life" (Proverbs 4:23). True wisdom recognizes that we must guard our heart and cultivate our affectivity as well.

It's also significant that we learn to objectify our emotions. The essence of EQ relies on how well we observe, discern and channel our emotions. When affectivity is well cultivated, it's easier to control. When we control our emotion reasonably well, we become empathetic toward others. When we motivate ourselves, we also become skillful in motivating others.

Life isn't about competing with others. Rather, it's about competing with ourself. Ruling ourself and our mind is incomparably more important than gaining the whole world. We might even say that life consists in overcoming negative emotions. Proverbs speaks to this matter. "One who is slow to anger is better than the mighty, / and one whose temper is controlled [is mightier] than one who captures a city" (Proverbs 16:32).

PRACTICE

Find the Right Environment

For me the right environment for memorizing is my study. It's a quiet, well-lit place with a comfortable chair and a desktop that's clear. But for you the right environment may be just the opposite: a noisy, ill-lit place with a broken chair and a tabletop covered with ten years of loose paper. The right environment for you is the one that fits like a glove.

For me, neither a full stomach nor an empty one helps my concentration. But for you anything from a long-term fast to a seven-course banquet may be appropriate.

The right environment may be found in your house or apartment; it may be in your basement or garage. If a local church has a room, that would be nice.

I began memorizing Scripture as soon as I was converted to the faith as a very young man. I grew up in a church that emphasized memorization. Youth dedication services throughout the church year included Scripture recitation. But the pastor didn't limit the memorization program to adults; children and college groups had their own programs.

Church model. A church that puts high priority on discipleship teaches Scripture memorization. No doubt there are many model churches, but the one that sticks out in my mind is the SaRang Community Church in Seoul, Korea. Every lay leader is trained not only in topical memorization of Scripture but also in total recall of Romans 8. The senior pastor memorizes, and everyone else in the church feels they should too.

Corporate model. In the workplace, E-land Trading Company may be considered a model of Scripture memorization. Founder and CEO of the company Sung Soo Park memorizes Scripture, concentrating on passages pertaining to stewardship in the workplace; his example isn't lost on his employees. Another example is Won Hak Yeo of Kyujang Christian Publishing Company, who runs a clinic to motivate and train a lifestyle of memorizing the Word.

Family model. Evangelical pastor Charles Swindoll says his mother mightily influenced him in Scripture memorization. While he was still a child, she challenged him to memorize the Word. For every verse he memorized, she'd memorized two; for each chapter, she'd memorize two. She kept her promise faithfully. He learned Scripture painlessly.

Finding a partner for this lifestyle is wise. If you are married, reciting the Word with your spouse and children at home would be the greatest environment of all.

In his book *Growing Strong in the Seasons of Life*, Swindoll emphasizes the importance of memorizing the Word. "I know of no other single practice in the Christian life more rewarding, practically speaking, than memorizing Scripture. That's right. No other single discipline is more useful and rewarding than this. No other single exercise pays greater spiritual dividends!"

Ministry and mission models. Perhaps the best known group environment for memorizing the Word has been such parachurch ministries and mission organizations as Campus Crusade, the Navigators, InterVarsity Christian Fellowship and Joy Mission.

But the most important environment for memorizing the Word is our inner being. Seek the help of the Holy Spirit; he alone enables us to be truly and indeed totally intrigued by the Word.

9

OVERCOMING ANXIETY

Do not worry about anything, but in everything by prayer and
supplication with thanksgiving let your requests be made known to God.
And the peace of God, which surpasses all understanding,
will guard your hearts and your minds in Christ Jesus.

PHILIPPIANS 4:6-7

Memorizing Scripture helps us become people of God. It makes us submissive to his word. It increases the quality of our intellectual life. Choosing what to think is such a blessing, such a gift, such a reward.

Anxiety is a devilry. We must be perpetually on guard against it. It comes from inability to make up our mind. When we finally decide, being anxious, we end up making the wrong decision. Learning Scripture by heart, on the other hand, is a form of spiritual exercise and intellectual discipline that encourages us to make the right choice.

Spirituality has depth; it knows how to live fully in the present; its essence is the "here and now." It's not bogged down by the past and doesn't cringe with anxiety about the future. Living fully in the present means living in a focused way; it also means living faithfully even though we don't know what the future holds.

We humans have limitations; we can't detach ourselves from the past. But still, we can choose to live in the present without being enslaved by the past. To learn from the past, God gave us memory; to live wisely in the present, God let us learn from our mistakes. We have a choice now. We can worry about the future, or we can keep one eye on the present and the other eye on the future.

Anxiety is a major obstacle when we try to dream the great dream. It stifles risk-taking, drowns the pioneering spirit, rules out challenges. If we're crippled by anxiety, we'll slowly weaken until we can no longer lift a finger on our own behalf.

Anxiety will also attack our physical health. We already know that many diseases have anxiety components. Sometimes the anxiety about an illness is more serious than the illness itself. It removes the sense of happiness and satisfaction, two affections of the soul that sustain many positive and healthy emotions. But left to itself, anxiety will replace them with nervousness and insecurity.

Anxiety tends to becomes habitual. It develops into a habit of mind that makes the wrong choice, walks the wrong path. Bad habits eventually turn into addiction that will topple the strongest personality. Remember, bad habits are like industrious beetles who, given time enough, can bring a whole tree down.

One successful antidote to anxiety is cherishing Scripture in our heart.

In the Sermon on the Mount, Jesus has some words of consolation for his followers.

> Do not worry about your life, what you will eat or what you will drink, or about your body, what you will wear. Is not life more than food, and the body more than clothing? Look at the birds of the air; they neither sow nor reap nor gather into barns, and yet your heavenly Father feeds them. Are you not of more value

than they? And can any of you by worrying add a single hour to your span of life? And why do you worry about clothing? Consider the lilies of the field, how they grow; they neither toil nor spin, yet I tell you, even Solomon in all his glory was not clothed like one of these. But if God so clothes the grass of the field, which is alive today and tomorrow is thrown into the oven, will he not much more clothe you—you of little faith? Therefore do not worry, saying, "What will we eat?" or "What will we drink?" or "What will we wear?" For it is the Gentiles who strive for all these things; and indeed your heavenly Father knows that you need all these things. But strive first for the kingdom of God and his righteousness, and all these things will be given to you as well.

So do not worry about tomorrow, for tomorrow will bring worries of its own. Today's trouble is enough for today. (Matthew 6:25-34)

Later, Jesus tries to allay the anxiety of his followers in the garden of Gethsemane. "Do not let your hearts be troubled. Believe in God, believe also in me" (John 14:1).

The apostle Paul says, "Do not worry about anything, but in everything by prayer and supplication with thanksgiving let your requests be made known to God. And the peace of God, which surpasses all understanding, will guard your hearts and your minds in Christ Jesus" (Philippians 4:6-7).

When the Enemy begins a frontal assault against us, we must bring forward a weapon capable of resisting all anxiety. This is none other than the sword of the Spirit, the Word of God.

10

Enjoying Peace

Let the peace of Christ rule in your hearts,
to which indeed you were called in the one body. And be thankful.

COLOSSIANS 3:15

Memorizing Scripture invites the blessings of peace into your heart. Anxiety, on the other hand, disinvites the peace of God. It divides the mind, it chokes the very life out of us, and it produces insecurity and fear. The Word of God in the heart, on the other hand, drives away this darkness and replaces it with peace.

Whenever I experience anxiety, fear or feelings of insecurity, I turn to Scripture, returning prayerfully to where I've been memorizing last. But before I begin the process again, I say that lovely prayer from Philippians.

> Do not worry about anything, but in everything by prayer and supplication with thanksgiving let your requests be made known to God. And the peace of God, which surpasses all understanding, will guard your hearts and your minds in Christ Jesus. (Philippians 4:6-7)

Whenever anxiety strikes us, we ought to analyze its cause. Quite often it turns out to be trivial. But if we don't pursue the cause, if we let it remain hidden, if we don't defang the viper, it will poison us to death.

At times anxiety brings with it a heavy burden. This too can be removed when we hand it off to God in prayer. The apostle Peter assures us of this: "Cast all your anxiety on him, because he cares for you" (1 Peter 5:7). Yes, he takes our load upon himself.

But if our anxiety is rooted in disobedience to God, there's no other way but to listen to Isaiah:

O that you had paid attention to my commandments!
    Then your prosperity would have been like a river,
    and your success like the waves of the sea. (Isaiah 48:18)

Listen to Isaiah again. "Those of steadfast mind you keep in peace— / in peace because they trust in you" (Isaiah 26:3).

Whenever anxiety strikes, we should approach God with a thankful heart and pray some verses we've already memorized. Then he'll replace our fears with his peace. How exactly does this transfer work? It surpasses all understanding.

I pray that you'll make Paul's advice to the Colossians your own: "Let the peace of Christ rule in your hearts, to which indeed you were called in the one body. And be thankful" (Colossians 3:15).

PRACTICE

Divide and Conquer

The old adage "divide and conquer" applies to memorizing Scripture just as it does to eating a pie; this is especially true when the verses are long and unmanageable.

Calvin Coolidge put it another way: "We cannot do everything at once, but we can do something at once" (as quoted in *Wisdom for the Soul* by Larry Chang). In other words, all we have to do is connect what we've conquered in small parts.

Set realistic but challenging goals. Our hearts gravitate toward what is possible and shun what's impossible. At the same time, we also like to stretch ourselves beyond our reach to see what happens. The best thing to do is to take a humongous goal and divide it into manageable parts. Just as sand passes through an hourglass, one grain at a time, so it is with Scripture memorization. By progressing a little bit at a time we can memorize vast amounts of truth from God's Word.

One verse at a time. It's easy to recall the first and the last items learned. The middle part is always the most difficult to remember. When we hear a lecture or a sermon, we usually remember the striking illustration at the beginning and the brilliant summary at the end; the middle is something of a muddle.

It's easy to memorize the beginning and ending of a mile-long verse. Once that's done, we can add a little more from the beginning and a little more from the ending. When we repeat this process, we suddenly discover that we've memorized the monster.

A word of caution: During this whole process we must always keep the entire verse in mind. Otherwise, we'll be lumbering the trees without harvesting the forest.

11

STRENGTHENING THE HEART

Do not fear, for I am with you,

do not be afraid, for I am your God;

I will strengthen you, I will help you,

I will uphold you with my victorious right hand.

ISAIAH 41:10

All Christians, male and female alike, are called to spiritual warfare. The most important requirement for them as they face the battle is courage. Not necessarily physical courage but mental courage. All battles begin in the mind. If we can win there, we've already won in the field.

The greatest obstacle to victory, in war as in everything else, lies within. It's fear, plain and simple. Even a seasoned warrior like Joshua was afraid when Moses died; the task ahead of conquering Canaan was overwhelming. God had to issue a solemn command:

Be strong and courageous; for you shall put this people in possession of the land that I swore to their ancestors to give them. (Joshua 1:6).

Be strong and courageous; do not be frightened or dismayed, for
the LORD your God is with you wherever you go. (Joshua 1:9)

Please note that God repeated the words *be strong* to Joshua.
Holding fast to them and nothing else, Joshua finally got a handle
on his fear. God's promise to walk with him was enough; he knew
he'd be victorious. As with Joshua, God constantly exhorts us not to
fear. He has a mission for us too, and he'll walk with us until we
come to the end.

Courage is a common quality belonging to the victorious people
of God, but it's not the only one; confidence and conviction are com-
plementary qualities. They bring not only victory but also great re-
wards. The letter to the Hebrews confirms this. "Do not . . . abandon
that confidence of yours; it brings a great reward" (Hebrews 10:35).

How do we acquire these spiritual commodities? Through learning Scripture by heart and through faith, according to Paul: "Faith
comes from what is heard, and what is heard comes through the
word of Christ" (Romans 10:17).

Courage doesn't mean that a person has no fear. Rather, it's a response: keep advancing in spite of fear. It's the capacity to endure a
little longer. As American poet Ralph Waldo Emerson articulated,
courage enables all of us to endure for another five minutes. The very
resource for this kind of endurance is found in memorizing Scripture. One verse from Isaiah comes to mind:

Do not fear, for I am with you,
    do not be afraid, for I am your God;
I will strengthen you, I will help you,
    I will uphold you with my victorious right hand.
(Isaiah 41:10)

The words you commit to memory will sustain you.

Over and above that, the Spirit has the power to raise your inner
spirits; for some, that would be like breathing life into the dead.

12

IMPROVING THE POWER
OF LEARNING

Keep these words that I am commanding you today in your heart.
Recite them to your children and talk about
them when you are at home and when you are away,
when you lie down and when you rise.

DEUTERONOMY 6:6-7

People who have shaped history in the past and will shape it in the future live as perpetual learners. They regard knowledge to be as precious as life. Because they utilize information and knowledge wisely and well, they're in constant demand. These talented individuals don't merely possess knowledge of the past; they also produce knowledge for present and future use by others.

If we're to remain faithful to God's mission, we too must appreciate knowledge. A Christian leader must grow in his or her use of personal and financial resources, yes, but also of intellectual resources. People of God should also be known as perpetual learners, ever refining their learning skills if they expect to be spiritual leaders of the twenty-first century.

Some decades ago futurist Alvin Toffler predicted that "the illiterate in the twenty-first century is not one who cannot read or write, but one who lacks the skill to learn, refine, and relearn" (as quoted in *Learning by Heart* by Roland S. Barth). This distinction between the skilled and the unskilled is vital. It's like a scenario in which a motorist and a cyclist race toward the same destination; the difference is insignificant at first, but soon it will be enormous.

God's primary education principles for his people appear in Deuteronomy.

> Keep these words that I am commanding you today in your heart. Recite them to your children and talk about them when you are at home and when you are away, when you lie down and when you rise. (Deuteronomy 6:6-7)

This is the key to Israel's rise to prominence.

God goes on to remind Joshua, leader of the next generation, of the commandments spoken by Moses: "Be strong and courageous; for you shall put this people in possession of the land that I swore to their ancestors to give them" (Joshua 1:6). As one who was deepened by meditating on the Word, Joshua certainly qualifies as a perpetual learner.

There are four essential ingredients of successful learning: memory, synthesis, creativity and judgment. Memory is foundational. What is recalled may be synthesized and transformed. What is remembered may be compared and analyzed. All basic concepts and principles are grounded on memorization. Learning begins with remembering; no learning occurs without memory.

We lead a victorious or successful life when we can reflect and act on what we've learned.

Learning Scripture by heart cultivates the skill of memory and thereby promotes the skill of learning.

PRACTICE

Get It Right the First Time

When people memorize the Word for the first time, they get the drift of a passage and come close to getting the wording right. Having come so far, they feel delighted with their progress. But they shouldn't press on until they completely master the wording of the text. Nothing less than precision is acceptable.

Precise memorization, precise utilization. Initially, precision is difficult to achieve, but in the end it's worth the effort. When used in the ministry, the memorized verses, like polished instruments, sharpened swords, will be easier to review.

As the number of memorized verses increases, we gain greater confidence in our ability to recall them. Like a muscle, our memory strengthens with exercise. As it improves with Scripture, it'll improve in the other areas too.

Comprehension. In *The Mind Map Book*, Tony Buzan asserts that 50 percent of conversation in whatever language uses fewer than one hundred words. He claims, therefore, that if we memorize one hundred essential words in any foreign language, we have already achieved 50 percent of comprehension. Likewise knowing many of the core verses of Scripture will help us to comprehend the overall themes of the Bible.

Acquire knowledge, wisdom and skill. Language skills have something in common with word memorization. We memorize word spellings and the multiplication table. So also we should memorize the Scripture verses common to most believers.

Scripture memorization is more a matter of function than of intellect, more a matter of method than of courage. We need more than sheer courage in life; we need knowledge and wisdom, and skills to use them both.

13

DEVELOPING CONCENTRATION

Every day he was teaching in the temple. . . .
And all the people would get up early in the morning
to listen to him in the temple.

LUKE 21:37-38

Nothing is as indispensable in leading a victorious life as the power to concentrate. Success doesn't necessarily come to those who work hard; rather it comes to those who work in a focused way. When we learn Scripture by heart, we grow in the sanctified habit of concentration.

Concentration is the driving force behind all accomplishments. If we give our time simultaneously to many projects, it's unlikely that we'll make a great contribution to any one of them. But if we concentrate on digging one well until the water finally springs, this makes a real contribution.

We can't study without concentration. We can't cultivate the mind without concentration. We can't employ our memory or creativity without concentration. We can't solve problems without concentration. We can't memorize Scripture without concentration.

Memorizing Scripture begins with resolve, the resolve to focus. Our focus sets aside all other things for the sake of memorizing a brief passage. We mull over it, we muse over it, we meditate on it until we've made it our own. What we don't do is meditate on a hundred passages at one time in the hope of sudden mass memorization.

Greatness in humans is largely dependent on the power of habit. In his book *Joy at Work*, Dennis Bakke quotes the ancient Greek philosopher Aristotle: "We are what we repeatedly do. Excellence, therefore, is not an act but a habit." Which is another way of saying our present is dominated by habit, and our future will be determined by habit. (Hopefully our eulogist will focus more on our good habits than our bad ones.)

Habit isn't an overnight matter; it's a pattern, a lifestyle. No creature knows this as well as the spider tediously weaving a web of beauty and magnitude. The great Aesop would encourage us to follow the spider's way, one silken strand at a time. Hopefully, it will yield a holy and blessed life of faithfulness, but it may yield a life of destruction.

Jesus was the beneficiary of habit. He read Scripture in the synagogue (Luke 4:16), prayed early in the morning (Mark 1:35), prayed on high places (Luke 22:39). "Every day he was teaching in the temple, and at night he would go out and spend the night on the Mount of Olives, as it was called. And all the people would get up early in the morning to listen to him in the temple" (Luke 21:37-38).

When we commit ourselves to memorizing Scripture, we follow in Jesus' footsteps. We cultivate his lifestyle. We gather our wits and concentrate. Those who scatter their wits attempting many things with little effort will end up accomplishing few things of any value.

In memorizing Scripture we take an unmanageable task and divide it into smaller, manageable pieces. Thus we memorize Scripture not a book at a time, not a chapter at time, but a few verses at a time. Only when we have made them ours do we proceed to the next few verses.

Learning Scripture by heart cultivates concentration and reaps the inevitable wisdom.

14

STRENGTHENING THE WILL

If we endure, we will also reign with him;
if we deny him, he will also deny us.

2 TIMOTHY 2:12

A strong will is necessary to succeed in life; it propels us toward excellence and victory. In order to become God's people full of his fragrance, we must develop not only in mind and affections but also in will.

Will power is the operation of our mind to make a choice from many options. Will is the act of choosing or determining. It's the power to carry out a choice, put a choice into action. Which may be another way of saying, will is endurance.

Animals move only by impulse. Children act on impulse. Adults act on impulse too, but more often than not they act on will. Human weakness is not about failing too often; it's about giving up too soon. As long as we don't throw in the towel, we can always fight another round.

The most important character quality for success is endurance.

George Herbert Morrison said, "[We] win our victories by holding to it. We conquer not in any brilliant fashion—we conquer by continuing" (*Highways of the Heart*). He explained that the mark of every saint is a quiet but binding persistence.

Our will can be strengthened by training. The stronger our will, the easier learning Scripture by heart becomes. The more we memorize Scripture, the more steadfast and consistent we become.

Character may also be expressed as steadfast and consistent. We recognize these traits as signs of character in virtuous persons. They're not easily swayed by unfavorable circumstances. We feel we can trust them. They keep their word.

What moves the mind? It's spirituality. The spirit stimulates and motivates the mind toward action. Thus a wise person doesn't enforce an act; rather he or she motivates it through appropriate means. "If you want to build a ship," someone once said wisely, "do not call upon people to bring lumber, instructing them and assigning various duties. Instead, inspire them with an admiration to explore the mysterious and endless sea."

If we wish to strengthen the will, we should consider the mission God entrusted us with. Take enough time to set your mind on the goal of his calling. During such intense and sincere moments we'll receive burning hearts and strengthened wills.

Learning Scripture by heart has helped me strengthen my will. Every time I strove for a goal God gave me, I'd experience slippage; my will would weaken; I'd lose my grip.

To recover, I'd turn to the words of Jesus: "No one who puts a hand to the plow and looks back is fit for the kingdom of God" (Luke 9:62).

Other Scripture passages have strengthened me from time to time:

My soul takes no pleasure in anyone who shrinks back. (Hebrews 10:38)

We call blessed those who showed endurance. You have heard

of the endurance of Job, and you have seen the purpose of the Lord, how the Lord is compassionate and merciful. (James 5:11)

I endure everything for the sake of the elect, so that they may also obtain the salvation that is in Christ Jesus, with eternal glory. (2 Timothy 2:10)

If we endure, we will also reign with him; if we deny him, he will also deny us. (2 Timothy 2:12)

When we keep these words in our heart, they'll strengthen us on the road to victory.

PRACTICE

Use Index Cards

A simple index card is an invaluable tool when it comes to memorizing Scripture; it's easily accessible wherever we are. Packets of cards with scriptural quotes on them may be purchased at Christian bookstores. The verses are systematically selected and arranged, and cased in portable plastic or leather wallets. These are good for beginners. I use small index cards as well as notebooks.

Patience. When I planted a church, I selected verses on the topic of patience and memorized the following passages from Paul to Timothy.

> For that very reason I received mercy, so that in me, as the foremost, Jesus Christ might display the utmost patience, making me an example to those who would come to believe in him for eternal life. (1 Timothy 1:16)

> As for you, man of God, shun all this; pursue righteousness, godliness, faith, love, endurance, gentleness. (1 Timothy 6:11)

> I endure everything for the sake of the elect, so that they may also obtain the salvation that is in Christ Jesus, with eternal glory. (2 Timothy 2:10)

> The Lord's servant must not be quarrelsome but kindly to everyone, an apt teacher, patient. (2 Timothy 2:24)

Be persistent whether the time is favorable or unfavorable; convince, rebuke, and encourage, with the utmost patience in teaching. (2 Timothy 4:2)

While memorizing these passages, it occurred to me that the first mark of a biblical leader is patience, endurance and long-suffering.

Paul puts his finger on patience. "The signs of a true apostle were performed among you with utmost patience, signs and wonders and mighty works" (2 Corinthians 12:12).

Furthermore, Paul begins and ends his lengthy definition of love with words about patience. "Love is patient. . . . It . . . endures all things" (1 Corinthians 13:4-7).

Early on, each time I struggled with patience, I was encouraged by recalling and reciting these verses; they were handwritten on index cards inserted in my Bible.

15

CULTIVATING OURSELVES

And he said to them,
"Follow me, and I will make you fish for people."

MATTHEW 4:19

The Lord gave a primer on education to the Israelites; in effect, they had to perpetually develop themselves. Hence, the Israelites believed that if you give a fish to your children, you've fed them for one day. But if you teach them to fish, you've given them a livelihood. In modern terms, they gave their children a watch rather than telling them the time of day.

Learning Scripture by heart is like teaching children how to fish; it builds up the mind with discipline and spiritual knowledge, and that will affect our attitude toward life. Inevitably, people who have been trained this way discover their potential, grow in confidence and develop a healthy self-image.

Teachers transmit information. If they're good at it, they'll encourage students to learn on their own.

Good teachers also know that the ultimate goal of education isn't to make pupils dependent on teachers; it's to prepare them to continue their education long after they've left school.

Learning Scripture by heart is a case in point. One short-term effect is altering a bad course of action in our lives; a long-term effect is transforming our thinking. When things go wrong, the first thing we do is stop what we're doing and change our behavior, our environment or our friends. Before things substantially improve, though, we must change how we think. And we already have a mind-changing process in progress: memorizing Scripture verses.

Learning Scripture by heart affirms our potential. It also encourages us to influence others. In this vein, Walter Scott, a nineteenth-century Scottish novelist, said that the best education is one that benefits you. We must strive for a delicate balance between developing ourselves and ministering to others, but a lifelong learning program is absolutely necessary for continued influence in ministry.

If motivation is the key ingredient for success, then those of us who are already motivating ourselves through Scripture memorization have a great asset in achieving our larger goal. Completing a small task supplies us with the confidence to take on a larger challenge, and so on, in life's journey. But progress happens only where there's effort. There's no other way.

My prayer is that you take up the challenge of Scripture memorization.

16

PARENTING WISELY

My child, keep my words
and store up my commandments with you.

PROVERBS 7:1

Skillful parenting entails shepherding your children's heart. "Life flows out of the heart" according to Tedd Tripp, pastor and author of *Shepherding a Child's Heart*. "Parenting must be concerned with shepherding the heart. Parents must learn to read the problem in the heart of the child from observing the behavior, and help the child understand himself. In brief, parents should not merely reprimand a negative behavior, but learn wisdom to guide their heart."

Shepherding our children ultimately includes sowing God's Word in their young hearts. For us, Scripture memorization provides a treasury of God's words to choose from. Could there be any better way to inculcate biblical values in them?

We can validate this by citing the words of Jesus: "The good person out of the good treasure of the heart produces good, and the evil person out of evil treasure produces evil; for it is out of the abundance of the heart that the mouth speaks" (Luke 6:45).

Scripture inscribes a wealth of goodness upon the hearts of young and old alike. The book of Proverbs says much the same thing:

> My child, keep my words
>> and store up my commandments with you;
> keep my commandments and live,
>> keep my teachings as the apple of your eye;
> bind them on your fingers,
>> write them on the tablet of your heart. (Proverbs 7:1-3)

In the same chapter Proverbs tells us how to respond to the wayward woman.

> Say to wisdom, "You are my sister,"
>> and call insight your intimate friend,
> that they may keep you from the loose woman,
>> from the adulteress with her smooth words. (Proverbs 7:4-5)

When your children face temptations like these, the words of God hidden in their hearts will guard them.

These words of Scripture stress our role as parents; they teach our children how to cultivate their own hearts. "Keep your heart with all vigilance, / for from it flow the springs of life" (Proverbs 4:23).

We can help them to realize that this is possible only from meditating on Scripture and submitting their hearts to its prescriptions. We can teach them also to examine their hearts, repent of any sins and let the words of God richly dwell in their hearts.

A child's discovery of Scripture on his or her own has an enduring effect. Being taught Scripture by the Spirit himself has a permanent effect on a child. Memorizing the words of Scripture allows the Spirit to minister in everyday life situations, transforming their minds and life.

Assisting children to develop this habit of memorizing the Word has the added benefit of encouraging them to continue their education for the rest of their lives. Throughout history, this is what the great people of God have done.

If we're truly concerned about our children's future, we should set them a good example by memorizing Scripture ourselves.

PRACTICE

Arrange by Topic

The Enemy attacks us on many, well-organized fronts: doubt, anxiety, discouragement, fear, despair, hatred, lust, pride, jealousy, envy, guilt, failure, anger; the list is endless. In order to counterattack promptly and effectively, we need to arrange our memorized Scripture verses under a variety of headings and topics: assurance of salvation, hope, humility, guidance, encouragement, temptation, grace, victory; the list is endless.

Topical memory. *Topical Memory System* by the Navigators stresses two aspects:

First, topics are helpful for understanding and easy review.

Second, according to your need of occasion, these topics function as a "fishing hook" that draws the verse from memory. Topical arrangement helps the verses to occur in our minds as we witness, counsel, or prepare Bible studies and sermons.

With a topical framework, memorizing a psalm or a chapter becomes a manageable task. Here are some of my favorite examples:

- The good shepherd (John 10)
- The Lord's intercessory prayer (John 17)
- Luther's "Scripture of the Scriptures" (Romans 8)
- On love (1 Corinthians 13)

- On the resurrection (1 Corinthians 15)
- On faith (Hebrews 11)
- The Sermon on the Mount (Matthew 5–7).

I've even memorized whole books: Proverbs, Ephesians, 1 and 2 Timothy, Romans.

17

Nurturing Disciples

Very truly, I tell you, anyone who hears my word
and believes him who sent me has eternal life, and does not come
under judgment, but has passed from death to life.

JOHN 5:24

In the modern era, discipleship is often associated with the name Dawson Trotman, founder of the Navigators. As a young man working at a lumber mill, he began memorizing Scripture. He concentrated on twenty verses, thinking he could win a prize in a church youth group. But the prize wasn't what he thought it would be. Instead, one particular verse changed the course of his life.

In his brief autobiography *Born to Reproduce,* he describes what happened. He was walking to work at the lumber mill when one of the twenty verses he'd memorized, all to impress a pretty little blonde at the church, began to rattle around in his mind. "Verily, verily, I say unto you, He that heareth my word, and believeth on him that sent me, hath everlasting life" (John 5:24 KJV). The words "Hath everlasting life" especially caught his attention. He pulled out his pocket

New Testament, found the right place and checked out the rest of the verse: "And shall not come into condemnation; but is passed from death unto life." *I want some of that,* was his immediate reaction. And he prayed to the Lord, the first prayer he'd said as an adult, for ever-lasting life. The Lord responded. Young Trotman was born again.

Trotman came to Christ through memorizing Scripture. The practice nurtured his soul, as it will ours. As a new believer he committed one verse to memory every day for three years. At the end of that time, while driving a truck at the mill, he recalled a thousand verses.

When it came time for Trotman to nurture others, he recommended Scripture memorization; it was foundational to making disciples of others. "Becoming a believer," he once said, "is 10% compared to the other 90% which is nurture."

Trotman would often challenge new believers. "Do you really want to memorize the Word? What would prevent a person like you from doing it? Why do new believers attend church but remain generally ignorant of the Bible?"

We have much to learn from people like Trotman. Making a disciple out of a convert is necessary, but it's costly in time and effort. Scripture memorization is one of the costs the convert has to pay. It's long and it's hard, and as Trotman learned, there are no shortcuts in nurturing disciples.

The greatest example in making disciples through learning the Scriptures by heart is Jesus himself. He taught his disciples; they in turn taught others as they recalled the words their master had planted in their hearts. Like him they matured in the knowledge and meditation of truth.

18

MATURING AS A TEACHER

Whoever does [the commandments] and teaches them
will be called great in the kingdom of heaven.

MATTHEW 5:19

Anyone with a fervent desire to teach the Bible must study the Word deeply. Ezra provides a good example: "Ezra had set his heart to study the law of the LORD, and to do it, and to teach the statutes and ordinances in Israel" (Ezra 7:10).

A good Bible teacher teaches by example, as Jesus observes: "Whoever breaks one of the least of these commandments, and teaches others to do the same, will be called least in the kingdom of heaven; but whoever does them and teaches them will be called great in the kingdom of heaven" (Matthew 5:19).

A good Bible teacher should not only lead a worthy life but also learn Scripture by heart. A treasury of verses on deposit in a teacher's memory will greatly enhance the message.

The genius of humankind lies in making tools and utilizing them. A tool helps us achieve an objective with less effort in shorter time.

But a tool is useful only to those who've learned how to use it.

If the Bible is perceived in this way, as a map or a compass of life, a guidebook for victory and success in all matters of faith and practice, what better tool can there be in our hearts?

A good teacher will have free access to all of Scripture. He or she will not only know verses but also how to use them to benefit others. Spiritual progress occurs with the use or practice of Scripture. Professor Howard Hendricks aptly says, "The mark of spiritual maturity is not how much you understand, but how much you use" (*Living by the Book*).

The Bible wasn't given to us for preservation; it was given us to be lived, taught and proclaimed. "The word of God is living and active, sharper than any two-edged sword, piercing until it divides soul from spirit, joints from marrow; it is able to judge the thoughts and intentions of the heart" (Hebrews 4:12).

A trustworthy surgeon has access to a variety of surgical instruments and knows the function of each. The Word of God operates in much the same way; it has the power to remove the corruption and treat the sickness. In like manner, a good teacher commits to memory systematically and thematically a variety of Scripture verses, all with a view to personal discernment and the discernment of others.

PRACTICE

Make a Habit of It

When memorizing Scripture verses, we tend to read them silently with our eyes. It would be better if we read them aloud. After all, we'll be reciting them most of the time.

Remember how God had commanded Joshua, "This book of the law shall not depart out of your mouth" (Joshua 1:8). Keeping this command will yield incredible power in our lives. If indeed our language is transformed by the Scriptures, we will remove huge stumbling blocks in our lives (Mark 11:23).

The following suggestions come from the Navigators' *Topical Memory System.**

As you start to memorize a verse:

- Read in your Bible the context of the verse.

- Try to gain a clear understanding of what the verse actually means. You may want to read it in other Bible translations or paraphrases to get a better grasp of the meaning.

- Read the verse several times thoughtfully, aloud or in a whisper. This will help you grasp the verse as a whole. Each time you read it, say the reference, the verse, then the reference again.

- Discuss the verse with God in prayer, and continue to seek his help for success in Scripture memory.

While you are memorizing a verse:

- Say the verse aloud as much as possible.

- Learn the reference first.

- After learning the reference, learn the first phrase of the verse. Once you have learned the reference and first phrase and have repeated them correctly several times, add more phrases one by one.

- Think about how the verse applies to you and your daily circumstances.

- Always include the references as part of the verse as you learn and review it. Repeat the reference both before and after the verse.

After you can quote the verse correctly:

- You'll find it helpful to write out the verses. This deepens the impression in your mind.

- Review the verse immediately after learning it, and repeat it frequently in the next few days. This is crucial for fixing the verse firmly in mind, because of how quickly we tend to forget something we've recently learned.

- Review! Review! Review! Repetition is the best way to engrave the verses on your memory.

How to review memory verses with someone else:

- Follow this procedure: If the memory verses are written on cards, one person holds the other person's verse cards and reads the reference of the first card. (If the verses aren't written out, just use the Bible.) The other person then repeats the reference and goes on to quote the entire verse, with the reference again at the end. Then go on to other verses in the same way.

- First review the memory verses you know best.

- Recite your verses clearly, but not too rapidly, just so you can be easily understood.

- Make it your goal to repeat each verse word perfect.
- While the other person is quoting his or her verses, be helpful and encouraging. Do all you can to ensure success.
- When the other person makes a mistake, signal this to him or her by shaking your head or saying no. Give verbal help only if asked.
- Once the other person has realized the mistake, have him or her repeat the entire verse perfectly before going on.

Memorizing and reviewing Scripture with one or more friends will provide mutual encouragement as well as opportunities to discuss difficulties in memorization. You will also be helped by having someone with whom to share how God is using the verses in your life.

There are two rules for the foundation for a successful Scripture memory program:

1. Consistently memorize new verses each week.
2. Follow a daily program of reviewing the verses you have already memorized.

If memorizing Scripture becomes too routine, don't get discouraged. The process of recording Scripture on your mind and heart does have a mechanical aspect. It requires certain methods and a great deal of perseverance. But as long as the process of imprinting God's Word on your heart is moving forward, these Scriptures will be continually available for life-giving work.

There are helpful things you can do, however, if your Scripture memory program begins to seem lifeless. Try spending more time going over your verses in prayer and meditation. Also begin using the verses in your conversations or in letters. New freshness can come through sharing the Scriptures with others.

Keep in mind that memorizing and meditating on the Scriptures is a practical way of making them available to the Holy Spirit to use in your life.

---

*From the *Topical Memory System* (Colorado Springs: NavPress, 1969, 1981, 2006), pp. 15, 16, 19, 43.

19

Dialoguing Well

A word fitly spoken
is like apples of gold in a setting of silver.

PROVERBS 25:11

There are many types of dialogue: dialogue with God, dialogue between nations, dialogue between characters in a dramatic presentation. In this chapter *dialogue* means a conversation, a one-on-one exchange on a matter of some importance.

Pastors and priests, spiritual guides and directors should be able to hold a decent conversation with someone who needs or asks for help. In such a conversation many important if subtle things happen: teaching, persuasion, encouragement.

There are several things to notice.

First, language is powerful. The book of Proverbs has known this for thousands of years.

From the fruit of the mouth one's stomach is satisfied;
   the yield of the lips brings satisfaction.
Death and life are in the power of the tongue,
   and those who love it will eat its fruits. (Proverbs 18:20-21)

Our recognition of the power of language comes rather easily, but our capacity to use it comes rather slowly. The Greek philosopher Aristotle knew this distinction. "It is not enough to know what to say but it is also necessary to know how to say it." The difference between right and wrong use of language is comparable to a soothing balm and an irritating rash.

Second, all conversational dialogue is subject to the golden rule. Jesus said as much: "In everything do to others as you would have them do to you; for this is the law and the prophets" (Matthew 7:12). With this in mind, we should engage in a conversation with all possible courtesy toward the other person and his or her issues, whether we like them or not.

Third, decent, well-seasoned conversation may depend more on character than skill. As Joseph Addison, founder of *The Spectator* magazine, once noted, "There is no conversation so agreeable as that of the man of integrity, who hears without any intention to betray, and speaks without any intention to deceive." Pretentious words will never move a human heart. Love expressed or implied in truthful words will move mountains.

Fourth, timing is an age-old component of every successful significant conversation. "To make an apt answer is a joy to anyone, / and a word in season, how good it is!" (Proverbs 15:23). Once again, "A word fitly spoken / is like apples of gold in a setting of silver" (Proverbs 25:11). And untimely words often produce negative results:

Whoever blesses a neighbor with a loud voice,
    rising early in the morning,
    will be counted as cursing. (Proverbs 27:14)

Fifth, discernment plays a part in every seasoned conversation. More important than timeliness, word choice should be appropriate to the other person and the issue being discussed. American humorist Mark Twain recognized this: "The difference between the almost right word and the right word is really a large matter—'tis the difference between the lightning bug and the lightning" (*Mark Twain's Religion*).

Sixth, the ultimate goal in our important one-on-one conversations is to relate to another human being at a deeper level than we have in the past. The exchange may be intellectual, but it may take an emotional turn at any time.

In all of these aspects, learning Scripture by heart sharpens, seasons and softens our conversational skills.

20

OFFERING
SPIRITUAL COUNSEL

Morning by morning [the Lord] wakens—
wakens my ear
to listen as those who are taught.

ISAIAH 50:4

Memorizing Scripture has helped me understand human nature, to see our weakness as Isaiah did: "a bruised reed . . . / and a dimly burning wick" (Isaiah 42:3). Meditating on Scripture helped me to see the reality of original sin and the temptation of the enemy.

Scripture has taught me also that life is neither easy nor fair. Its seasons ebb and flow. There are good times and bad times, times when humanity suffers guilt and inferiority, pained by wounds deep in the soul. The problem is much deeper and complex than it appears on the surface. Some aren't reconciled with their past; some live with emotional scars.

I've learned too that the Lord is our healer, that true healing begins in our souls, that the Spirit operates through his Word. These

principles, which are based on the reality of the soul and the rugged-
ness of spiritual battle, are unknown to unbelieving counselors but
well known to us believers.

As a spiritual counselor I affirm time and again that scriptural
wisdom is the essence of good counseling. In this regard I'm reminded of Jesus' word to his disciples: "The Advocate, the Holy Spirit,
whom the Father will send in my name, will teach you everything,
and remind you of all that I have said to you" (John 14:26).

The obvious lesson is that the Spirit will use those Scripture passages that the counselor has already committed to memory. This
doesn't negate instances when the Spirit teaches wisdom beyond
what we've learned, but generally speaking he prefers to work co-
operatively with our efforts.

Discernment, much of which we learn from memorizing Scripture, is essential to effective counseling; it helps us identify the spiritual source of a problem. But we must listen attentively to the people
who come to us with their troubles. Listening is the first step in the
healing process.

The value of listening has been affirmed by Dr. Paul Tournier, a
Swiss physician who happened to be a Christian. "No one comes to
know himself through introspection or in the solitude of his personal diary. Rather, it is in dialog with his meeting other people" (*To
Understand Each Other*).

Tournier went on to say that doctors should help their patients
gain general self-knowledge even while they're helping them discern
their particular problems.

When spiritual doctors identify problems, they wisely tell patients
what they need to know, not what the patients want to hear. Helping
the spiritual doctors do so is the Spirit, who will pick and choose
verses from our memory that will fit the case.

The prophet Isaiah knew what to do millennia ago, and we would
do well to emulate him today.

> The Lord GOD has given me
>   the tongue of a teacher,

that I may know how to sustain
   the weary with a word.
Morning by morning he wakens—
   wakens my ear
     to listen as those who are taught. (Isaiah 50:4)

PRACTICE

Determine Topic, Reference, Word

Before we start memorizing a verse, it is helpful to determine its heading or topic and note the chapter and verse reference. Later, if we don't remember the exact words, we can still quickly look the verse up.

Moreover, memorizing the chapter and verse reference before and after each Scripture files them away for easy retrieval.

Memorized Scripture verses make it just that much easier for the Holy Spirit to communicate with us, to guide and instruct us.

Certainly, the more Scripture we memorize, the less dependent we become on the reference books. But we will never memorize enough Scripture to free us from our happy dependence on Bible dictionaries and commentaries.

21

BECOMING AN EVANGELIST

Always be ready to make your defense to anyone who
demands from you an accounting for the hope that is in you;
yet do it with gentleness and reverence.

1 PETER 3:15-16

God wills that the lost should receive eternal life through faith in Jesus Christ. Jesus says, "This is indeed the will of my Father, that all who see the Son and believe in him may have eternal life; and I will raise them up on the last day" (John 6:40).

I consider it a privilege to be among those used by God in this work of evangelism. Certainly, some of us are more gifted than others, but all saints should participate in this work and holy burden, the Great Commission given by the Lord Jesus.

Perhaps none was more gifted than the apostle Paul. And yet at times he was full of anxiety: "Woe to me if I do not preach the gospel!" (1 Corinthians 9:16 NIV). He expressed the same sentiment in a letter to Timothy. "Now the Spirit expressly says that in later times some will renounce the faith by paying attention to deceitful spirits and teachings of demons, through the hypocrisy of liars whose consciences are seared with a hot iron" (1 Timothy 4:1-2).

Evangelism is God's concern. "For since, in the wisdom of God, the world did not know God through wisdom, God decided, through the foolishness of our proclamation, to save those who believe" (1 Corinthians 1:21).

Paul called his efforts in this regard "foolish," yet no other apostle or disciple has been better prepared. What he meant was that his efforts, when compared to Christ's, were very small indeed.

Equipping ourself with the Word is essential to evangelism. Such preparation not only is wise but also pleases the Lord. "In your hearts sanctify Christ as Lord. Always be ready to make your defense to anyone who demands from you an accounting for the hope that is in you; yet do it with gentleness and reverence" (1 Peter 3:15-16).

Sharing the gospel with an inquirer inevitably involves some measure of presentation, persuasion and defense. In each of these a background of Scripture memorization gives us versatility in our dialogue. For instance, we can lead the unbeliever to discover truths in a variety of Scripture passages, no matter what the inquiry.

In Acts, Stephen's proclamation of the gospel message before the Jewish council illustrates a thematic presentation from memory.

> Brothers and fathers, listen to me. The God of glory appeared to our ancestor Abraham. . . . At this time Moses was born, and he was beautiful before God. . . . Our ancestors had the tent of testimony in the wilderness, as God directed when he spoke to Moses, ordering him to make it according to the pattern he had seen. Our ancestors in turn brought it [tent of testimony] in with Joshua. . . . It was there until the time of David. . . . But it was Solomon who built a house for him. (Acts 7:2, 20, 44, 45, 47)

And, approaching a synagogue, "Paul went in, as was his custom, and on three sabbath days argued with them from the scriptures, explaining and proving that it was necessary for the Messiah to suffer and to rise from the dead, and saying 'This is the Messiah, Jesus whom I am proclaiming to you' " (Acts 17:2-3).

In fact, Paul was "held captive" by the word. "When Silas and Timothy arrived from Macedonia, Paul was occupied with proclaiming the word, testifying to the Jews that the Messiah was Jesus" (Acts 18:5).

In other words, Paul was so immersed in Scripture, he had time for little else. He lived, breathed and had his being in the written words of Scripture. And so should we, as far as we are able.

22

LIVING IN FAITH

Until all of us come to the unity of the faith
and of the knowledge of the Son of God, to maturity,
to the measure of the full stature of Christ.

EPHESIANS 4:13

Learning Scripture by heart is critical in the disciple-making process. Granted, this isn't easy, but every disciple-maker should stress this discipline. Indeed, it's inconceivable that anyone could claim to follow a master but can't remember the master's teaching—yet it happens.

The apostle John quotes Jesus on this basic requirement. "If you continue in my word, you are truly my disciples" (John 8:31). This explicit teaching lays the foundation for all who seek to follow him.

According to Paul, the goal of discipleship won't be reached "until all of us come to the unity of the faith and of the knowledge of the Son of God, to maturity, to the measure of the full stature of Christ" (Ephesians 4:13).

In the next verse Paul tells us how to achieve all this. "We must no longer be children, tossed to and fro and blown about by every wind of doctrine, by people's trickery, by their craftiness in deceitful scheming" (Ephesians 4:14).

The instability he speaks of comes from the latest fads in doctrine, spiritual direction and church management. But why do people slip so easily? Quite simply, it's due to a lack of discernment and of education. We need to have a strong foundation of the core doctrines of Christianity. Accompanying that should be a systematic study of Scripture, which includes memorization of key Scripture passages that we can confidently recall and rely on.

Usually a person committed to memorizing Scripture on a regular basis is a disciplined thinker. Over a period of time he or she has trained to probe deeply into the truths of Scripture, finding a coherent and unified biblical worldview.

This also explains why the faith of these individuals can't be easily shaken. They regard the trials of life as opportunities to learn more from and commit themselves more deeply to Scripture. Such an attitude is biblical, rigorous and submitted to the authority of Christ.

Our maturity and immaturity can be discerned from our speech, understanding and thinking. Paul put it this way: "When I was a child, I spoke like a child, I thought like a child, I reasoned like a child; when I became an adult, I put an end to childish ways" (1 Corinthians 13:11).

Of course, we shouldn't undermine the childlike virtues of purity and humility, but children are always up to mischief of one sort or another, as Proverbs is quick to remind us: "Folly is bound up in the heart of a [child], / but the rod of discipline drives it far away" (Proverbs 22:15).

I sincerely believe that learning Scripture by heart is useful for teaching, rebuking and correcting, no matter what the age. Paul puts it this way. "All scripture is inspired by God and is useful for teaching, for reproof, for correction, and for training in righteousness" (2 Timothy 3:16).

Against the severest assaults of doubt, though, holding fast to the Word is the only sure refuge.

PRACTICE

Planning Our Memory Schedule

W e tend to be systematic in most areas of our lives, but when it comes to spiritual matters, we seem to fumble. When there's a time crunch, the first thing to go is Scripture memorization. Why? Because we put it right at the bottom of our list of spiritual priorities. Yet learning Scripture by heart should be right at the top. Charles Hummel, the author of *Freedom from Tyranny of the Urgent*, issued this warning: "Our greatest danger is letting the urgent things crowd out the important ones."

Scheduling time for memorizing. It's helpful to set aside a regular time every day to review our memory verses. For many people early morning hours are ideal. My best times are just before I go to bed and just after I wake up.

During the work day I have virtually no free time. Yet I can always find a few minutes here and there—on a bus, subway, plane, during break times, even while waiting for food at a restaurant.

Planning to memorize the Word is as important as memorizing itself. Paul Tournier says, "The yield of our life does not depend so much on the number of things that we do, but more on the quality of self-giving we put into each thing" (quoted in *The Sense of the Call* by Marva Dawn).

23

OVERCOMING TEMPTATION

I treasure your word in my heart,
so that I may not sin against you.

PSALM 119:11

It's more difficult to overcome temptation in good times than in bad times. That's what happened to King David; he fell into the sin of his life at the peak of his prosperity. Prosperity corrupts. Austerity, on the other hand, tends to purify. It is as if the latter carries the seed of success, and the former, that of defeat.

Temptation begins not from without but from within. The seed of temptation doesn't enter from outside but from within. That seed beckons temptations from within us. A polluted pool of water attracts flies; our corrupt desires draw plague-like infections. According to the letter of James, "One is tempted by one's own desire, being lured and enticed by it" (James 1:14).

To be tempted, therefore, implies that we were drawn by our desire toward deception. James continues. "When that desire has conceived, it gives birth to sin, and that sin, when it is fully grown, gives birth to death" (James 1:15).

It's not that our basic desires are illegitimate; they're just moving in the wrong direction. They entail unjustified means at the right time or justified means at the wrong time.

The proper response to temptation is discernment based on memorized Scripture verses. The proper strategy is a matter of stockpiling these verses before a riotous and radiant temptation assaults and overwhelms us.

When temptation becomes intense, we're unable to see the consequences of sin clearly: "A prostitute's fee is only a loaf of bread, / but the wife of another stalks a man's very life" (Proverbs 6:26).

Temptation starts as a small matter. We hardly notice that it's serious until it's tripped us up in public. When Peter betrayed the Lord, it wasn't before a host of Roman soldiers but in front of a slave girl.

A helpful early warning about an incoming temptation comes from the Song of Songs.

Catch us the foxes,
the little foxes,
that ruin the vineyards—
for our vineyards are in blossom. (Song of Solomon 2:15)

What withstands the treachery and the tenacity of temptation? Only the divine words in our heart can come to our aid, sharply discerning the good from the bad.

In the Psalms we find the following insight about Joseph, who, when he was a slave, triumphed over temptation. "Until what he had said came to pass, / the word of the LORD kept testing him" (Psalm 105:19). Since his mind's eye had been trained by the Word, he could look to God at the critical moment of temptation.

Psalm 119 contains two helpful verses echoing the credibility of the Word against temptation.

How can young people keep their way pure?
By guarding it according to your word. (v. 9)

I treasure your word in my heart,
    so that I may not sin against you. (v. 11)

Nailed upon our minds' temple, the Word of God will guard us with its holy presence.

24

FINDING VICTORY
IN SPIRITUAL WARFARE

Take the shield of faith, with which you will be able to quench
all the flaming arrows of the evil one. Take the helmet of salvation,
and the sword of the Spirit, which is the word of God.

EPHESIANS 6:16-17

If we're truly Christian disciples, we're equipped with a biblical worldview. We may have varying degrees of knowledge concerning spiritual realities and phenomena, but we all agree on one thing. We live in a fair field of flowers while spiritual warfare rages around us.

Since before time and recorded history, the Holy Spirit has been at war with the enemy. It is no wonder then that from the moment of faith in Jesus Christ, the Holy Spirit dwells in us Christians and opens our eyes to the realities of spiritual warfare.

No wonder Paul said, "Our struggle is not against enemies of blood and flesh, but against the rulers, against the authorities, against the cosmic powers of this present darkness, against the spiritual forces of evil in the heavenly places" (Ephesians 6:12).

Satan is the deceiver, the beguiler, the schismatic, the one who brings death and destruction to humanity through sin. Jesus is the redeemer, who, among his many chores on earth, was to destroy the works of this enemy. "Everyone who commits sin is a child of the devil; for the devil has been sinning from the beginning. The Son of God was revealed for this purpose, to destroy the works of the devil" (1 John 3:8).

The apostle Peter also warns of this. "Discipline yourselves, keep alert. Like a roaring lion your adversary the devil prowls around, looking for someone to devour. Resist him, steadfast in your faith, for you know that your brothers and sisters in all the world are undergoing the same kinds of suffering" (1 Peter 5:8-9).

How do we become victorious in spiritual warfare? By following the example of Jesus. In Matthew 4:1-11, Jesus spits out at the enemy the words "It is written," then quotes from Deuteronomy. That is to say, he parries the attempt by quoting Scripture. He does it not once, but three times. In the same gospel we also find these comforting words: "That evening they brought to him many who were possessed with demons; and he cast out the spirits with a word, and cured all who were sick" (Matthew 8:16).

Therefore, we can conclude that Jesus studied Hebrew Scriptures; indeed he memorized them and was able to recall appropriate verses when he was under attack.

The enemy very often attacks us not only through our thoughts but also through our emotions. Jesus saw that happen to one of his apostles. "The devil had already put it into the heart of Judas son of Simon Iscariot to betray him" (John 13:2).

When the enemy assaults us, he has such weapons in his arsenal as doubt, fear, confusion, discouragement, guilt, inferiority, incompetence, lust and anxiety. As a defensive weapon, Paul made this recommendation: "Take the shield of faith, with which you will be able to quench all the flaming arrows of the evil one" (Ephesians 6:16). As an offensive weapon Paul recommended "the helmet of salvation, and the sword of the Spirit, which is the word of God" (Ephesians 6:17).

None of the previous has any value unless the Word dwells in us. The apostle John aptly put it this way: "I write to you, children, / because you know the Father. / I write to you, fathers, because you know him who is from the beginning. / I write to you, young people, because you are strong / and the word of God abides in you, / and you have overcome the evil one" (1 John 2:14).

Let Scripture dwell in you. It's the key to overcoming the evil one. I urge you to commit Scripture to memory, to arrange them in your memory thematically and to use them often. You will begin to experience a vibrant and victorious intellectual life as a good steward of Christ.

PRACTICE

Understanding What We Memorize

Understanding is the shortcut to memorization; meaningfulness reinforces memory. It takes more time to fully comprehend what we're memorizing, but our understanding will be etched in our minds forever.

Understanding and inspiration. Understanding inspires; inspiration sustains. Of course, this would be true of the books we read, but it's especially true of Scripture memorization.

Discovery and observation. New insights inspire us; the more we're inspired, the better we remember. But we need the humility of a child before we can discover new insights. We can still delight in small discoveries. As Proverbs says, "Doing wrong is like sport to a fool, / but wise conduct is pleasure to a person of understanding" (Proverbs 10:23).

Ask questions while you observe. Careful observation leads to much discovery. Both before and after we memorize a verse, we should examine the context. We should ask questions, consult reference works, find the precise meaning. In "The Elephant's Child," British poet and journalist Rudyard Kipling has something to say on this point:

I keep six honest serving-men:
(They taught me all I know)
Their names are What and Why and When
And How and Where and Who.

Once we make careful observations aided by these questions, our interpretation and application of the text become easier.

We don't easily forget what we discover through our own questions. Our recollections of how we felt when we received answers to our questions in certain gatherings assure their longevity in our memory.

Personalizing the meaning. When I was planting the Logos Church in Los Angeles, I personally took to heart a verse from the Gospel of John. "Very truly, I tell you, the one who believes in me will also do the works that I do and, in fact, will do greater works than these, because I am going to the Father" (John 14:12).

Because I'd personalized this verse, I was able to remember and for a long time share this verse with people who came to our church. Through this verse the Lord Jesus gave me a great vision: he trusted me.

If we look at the context around this verse, we receive a richer meaning. The Lord promises to lead us so that we may do greater things by means of prayer (vv. 13-14). Moreover, he promises the Holy Spirit (v. 16), and he speaks of love (v. 15) as the proper motive for doing these greater things.

From these verses I understand that our vision to do great things should not be motivated by selfish ambition but by love; only through prayer and the Holy Spirit can we accomplish great deeds of the kingdom. These inspiring teachings had an impact on my heart and gave me encouragement during those trying times.

25

PREVAILING PRAYER

If you abide in me, and my words abide in you,
ask for whatever you wish, and it will be done for you.

JOHN 15:7

The greatest privilege of a Christian, adopted as a child of God, is prayer. Prayer is the key that unlocks heaven, at least according to Jesus: "I will give you the keys of the kingdom of heaven, and whatever you bind on earth will be bound in heaven, and whatever you loose on earth will be loosed in heaven" (Matthew 16:19). The key that unlocks heaven's gate refers to the work of the gospel through prayer.

Yes, prayer has power. Jesus speaks further about the power of prayer in the same Gospel. "Truly I tell you, whatever you bind on earth will be bound in heaven, and whatever you loose on earth will be loosed in heaven. Again, truly I tell you, if two of you agree on earth about anything you ask, it will be done for you by my Father in heaven" (Matthew 18:18-19).

Joseph and David in the Old Testament and Peter and Paul in the

New Testament were given the keys of the kingdom. They too opened hearts through prayer and routed the force of darkness and evil spirits.

Such is the power and duty endowed to every Christian through prayer. John Bunyan, a seventeenth-century writer and Christian, once said this: "Prayer is the shield to the soul, a sacrifice to God and a scourge for Satan" (*The Complete Works of John Bunyan*). Making much the same point is Dick Eastman, president of Every Home for Christ and originator of the Change the World School of Prayer. "Satan is terrified at the weakest Christian kneeling at the altar of prayer."

What kind of prayer terrifies the enemy? What kind of prayer truly prevails with God? It's prayer standing on the promises God has made on our behalf. That's why we must study them and memorize them first. Afterward, we pray these promises. God's waiting to answer our faithful prayers, and when he does, we can say "Amen."

Paul seconds this: "In [Jesus Christ] every one of God's promises is a 'Yes.' For this reason it is through him that we say the 'Amen' " (2 Corinthians 1:20).

When we meditate on this verse, we see that it relates to God's promise. It tells how Jesus personalized God's promise some millennia ago. Moreover, when we say "Amen," we glorify God through our prayers in Jesus' name. "Amen" is one of Jesus' names: "The words of the Amen, the faithful and true witness, the origin of God's creation" (Revelation 3:14). Our prayers in Jesus' name give glory to God. This is clear in John, who quotes Jesus to the same effect. "I will do whatever you ask in my name, so that the Father may be glorified in the Son" (John 14:13).

We can personally possess many of God's promises through memorizing his Word. This will help us to pray biblically; God always responds to biblical prayer. "If you abide in me, and my words abide in you, ask for whatever you wish, and it will be done for you" (John 15:7).

26

PREPARING FOR
SPIRITUAL DIFFICULTY

If you faint in the day of adversity,
your strength [is] small.

PROVERBS 24:10

In the ebb and flow of life, times of famine occasionally replace seasons of harvest; the same is true in the spiritual realm. A person who has committed to memory a wealth of Scripture is well prepared for such times. But even here the prophet Amos thinks we may not have prepared enough:

> The time is surely coming, says the Lord GOD,
>   when I will send a famine on the land;
> not a famine of bread, or a thirst for water,
>   but of hearing the words of the LORD. (Amos 8:11)

Along this line, Joseph is our model; he prepared for the seven-year famine. He had discerned this by interpreting Pharaoh's dream (Genesis 41:29-31) and advising him to prepare for these difficult times (Genesis 41:33-36).

The true test of spiritual wisdom lies in this capacity to foresee and prepare for times of dearth. According to Proverbs, however, "If you faint in the day of adversity, / your strength [is] small" (Proverbs 24:10). Proverbs also teaches us that strength in time of trouble comes from foresight. "The ants are a people without strength, / yet they provide [a year's worth of] food in the summer" (Proverbs 30:25).

Jacob DeShazer was an American pilot shot down in the first bombing of Tokyo during World War II and captured by the enemy. He'd grown up in a Christian home but never gave a serious thought to Jesus Christ. Now that he was confined to a solitary life, he had plenty of time to read the Bible, which he had in confinement. Within three weeks he realized he was a sinner before God and that Jesus' sacrificial death on the cross paid the penalty for his sins. He had encountered God through the Word and received Christ that day in the prison camp.

He knew his Bible would eventually be confiscated, so he began to memorize verses. He committed to memory 1 Corinthians 13, the great chapter on love. He meditated on these verses and realized that Christ's teaching on love extended to his enemies. These verses became a source of power and comfort during his fourteen-month confinement, and he was even able to love his guards, who tortured him through various means.

His example challenges us to wisely prepare ourselves for the day of trouble; we should keep the Word in store for ourselves. The Lord made the same point with Peter by asking a rhetorical question. "Who . . . is the faithful and prudent manager whom his master will put in charge of his slaves, to give them their allowance of food at the proper time?" (Luke 12:42).

The reason Jacob DeShazer could do this unthinkable thing—loving his captors—is that his soul was prepared for this season by memorizing Scripture. The Scriptures in Jacob's heart enabled him to overcome his fears and the brutal mistreatment.

PRACTICE

Meditation and Transformation

Our goal isn't memorizing as many Scripture verses as possible. It's conforming to the image of Jesus Christ. It's a pursuit of holiness to reach godliness. For this purpose we commit ourselves to be filled with the richness of God's Word. Transformation and maturity are more important than the quantity of Scripture memorized.

Applying the Word. We may begin applying the Word to our own special situation as soon as we meditate on the Word. Since the goal of meditation lies in obeying the Lord, meditation actually matures us in our inner character. About the importance of meditation Puritan preacher Thomas Watson says, "The reason we come away so cold from reading the Word is because we do not warm ourselves at the fire of meditation" (*The Bible and the Closet*).

Asking questions. Asking questions during meditation helps us to properly apply the Word, only this time, these are application questions not observation questions. The following seven questions have helped me over the years.

1. What new knowledge have I gained concerning God (the Father, the Son, the Holy Spirit)?

2. What new truth have I discovered?

3. What example should I follow?

4. What command should I obey?

5. What errors should I avoid?

6. What sins should I forsake?

7. What promises should I seek?

With regard to the second question, I have in mind particularly those truths that pertain to wisdom and insight for living, understanding humanity, life and the spiritual world, and so on. Scripture memorization connected to application yields significant influence on our lives.

Repetition. Since the Word of God is the sword of the Spirit, it's a weapon we must use. But more importantly, our lives need to be read in light of Scripture; we're healed by the Word as a surgical knife.

This is the meaning of Hebrews 4:12: "The word of God is living and active, sharper than any two-edged sword, piercing until it divides soul from spirit, joints from marrow; it is able to judge the thoughts and intentions of the heart."

If the Word of God can penetrate our thoughts and motives, David certainly testifies of this experience long ago:

> O LORD, you have searched me and known me.
> You know when I sit down and when I rise up;
>   you discern my thoughts from far away.
> You search out my path and my lying down,
>   and are acquainted with all my ways.
> Even before a word is on my tongue,
>   O LORD, you know it completely.
> You hem me in, behind and before,
>   and lay your hand upon me.
> Such knowledge is too wonderful for me;
>   it is so high that I cannot attain it.
>
> Where can I go from your spirit?
>   Or where can I flee from your presence? (Psalm 139:1-7)

When we understand and memorize God's Word, we experience a transformation that makes us transparent vessels that fulfill the Word in everyday life. The Word becomes incarnate in us and literally lives through us.

27

TRANSFORMING TRIALS

My brothers and sisters, whenever you face trials of any kind,
consider it nothing but joy, because you know that the
testing of your faith produces endurance;
and let endurance have its full effect, so that you may
be mature and complete, lacking in nothing.

JAMES 1:2-4

Another benefit of learning Scripture by heart is that it transforms trials into maturing opportunities.

The calendar year has four seasons, and life also has seasons, times of varying circumstances and stages. Solomon put it this way. "In the day of prosperity be joyful, and in the day of adversity consider; God has made the one as well as the other, so that mortals may not find out anything that will come after them" (Ecclesiastes 7:14).

Learning Scripture by heart prepares us to think clearly when spiritual times are hard. It forges a proper attitude, disposition and perspective. It keeps us nimble, resilient and sharp in our daily response.

Adversity plays no favorites. Everyone experiences trials and sufferings. Christians certainly aren't exempt, nor is Jesus himself. "Although he was a Son, he learned obedience through what he suffered" (Hebrews 5:8). It's good to be prepared for trials, for they can visit us numerous times.

Suffering is a crisis in life, a painful, even desperate experience. Yet in the suffering lies the great mystery. Some of us have been purified by the pain and risen above it; others have fallen, never to rise again. Keeping the Word in our heart helps.

Scripture sees trials in a positive way, but we look at them with the utmost puzzlement. On the other hand, if we have a glimpse of the meaning of pain, especially through memorized Scripture, we're more than capable of handling it.

Under spiritual duress I always turn to the letter of James: "My brothers and sisters, whenever you face trials of any kind, consider it nothing but joy, because you know that the testing of your faith produces endurance; and let endurance have its full effect, so that you may be mature and complete, lacking in nothing" (James 1:2-4).

God's will includes suffering, for the sake of growth. "Those whom he foreknew he also predestined to be conformed to the image of his Son, in order that he might be the firstborn within a large family" (Romans 8:29). God's actually purifying and training us.

Suffering is also our teacher: it produces teachable moments, and we're more ready to learn to obey. The psalmist puts it this way: "Before I was humbled I went astray, / but now I keep your word" (Psalm 119:67). In other words, suffering doesn't leave us in the same place; it moves us toward maturity, to the full measure of Christ.

Walking on the burning coals, with the help of Scripture in our hearts, generates joy and exhilaration. The psalmist shares his experience: "If your law had not been my delight, / I would have perished in my misery" (Psalm 119:92).

Let's not be paralyzed in the face of suffering; instead, let's seize the pain and see it as opportunity for growth.

PRACTICE

Memorize with an Eye on Use

Human beings are born with an inclination toward purpose. For this reason, we live with vigor only when we have a goal and purpose ahead of us. The same principle applies to memorizing the Word; we're most effective when we can imagine how we can make the most out of it.

Set goals. Setting different goals has been advantageous to me. When reading the Bible, devotionals or any other books, I think about how I'll use different insights I gain. Since I read topically, my interaction with the news, magazines and books has a direct bearing on the messages, lectures and articles I prepare.

For example, I set goals by themes weekly. Each week has a theme, and I find the verses that are related to that theme. Usually the weekly theme has to do with my sermon topic for the following week. As I prepare my sermon notes, I try to memorize all the verses that I use for my sermon. If the sermon topic is joy, then I start memorizing and meditating on the verses on the joy of the Lord. The index of this book includes some of my favorite verses by themes. I chose 1 Thessalonians 5:16-18 and 1 Peter 1:8-9 on the theme of joy. Even if there are ten or more verses, I try to memorize those verses before my sermon as long as they are related to the theme of the sermon.

My writing develops out of the verses that I memorized and meditated upon for the week. I write a short pastoral letter to my congregation every week, and a few other articles for Christian magazines and journals on spirituality. I don't mean to write out from the beginning. Instead, the writings come out naturally as a result of memorization and meditation on the Word of God.

Immediately put to use what you learn. Having many ways of using and sharing the insights that have blessed us isn't something we should be ashamed of. The alternative is keeping our insights to ourselves until we forget about them. Sharing what we've received immediately and repeatedly reinforces what we've learned.

You are a cherished instrument in his hand. Remember, the verses you memorize make you more valuable in God's service. The work of memorization is clearly meant to serve others, and you must pray for divine help in this regard. A passage from Howard Hendricks's book *Teaching to Change Lives* comes to mind:

> No matter how it makes you feel, if you want to minister to others, ask God first of all to minister to you. He wants to work through you—but he can't until he works in you. He'll use you as his instrument, but he wants to sharpen and cleanse that instrument so it becomes a more effective tool in his hands.

28

RECEIVING
DIVINE GUIDANCE

Trust in the LORD with all your heart,
and do not rely on your own insight.
In all your ways acknowledge him,
and he will make straight your paths.

PROVERBS 3:5-6

God wants to guide our lives because he loves us, not just occasionally but all of the time. When we let him do so, we're like trees planted by the water, lacking nothing. It's a scene right out of Isaiah:

> The LORD will guide you continually,
>   and satisfy your needs in parched places,
>   and make your bones strong;
> and you shall be like a watered garden,
>   like a spring of water,
>   whose waters never fail. (Isaiah 58:11)

Memorizing Scripture keeps spiritual guidance fresh and strong. One verse from Psalms comes immediately to mind. "Your word is a lamp to my feet / and a light to my path" (Psalm 119:105).

Likewise, David and Asaph express their desire to be guided by the Word:

> Lead me in your truth, and teach me,
>> for you are the God of my salvation;
>> for you I wait all day long. (Psalm 25:5)

Another psalm says, "You guide me with your counsel, / and afterward you will receive me with honor" (Psalm 73:24).

Proverbs also teaches how God's people ought not trust their own wisdom, which is the natural tendency when we neglect the Word.

> Trust in the LORD with all your heart,
>> and do not rely on your own insight.
> In all your ways acknowledge him,
>> and he will make straight your paths. (Proverbs 3:5-6)

Our experiences can be valuable sources of wisdom, but they can also mislead us. Peter knew all there was to know about fishing. One night, he caught nothing on one side of the boat; there was no need to try the other side. But when the Lord spoke, he swallowed his pride and tried anyway. Obeying the Lord brought more fish into the boat than it could hold. Peter's spiritual eyes were opened, and he saw who Jesus really was.

Reading God's Word every morning certainly provides us with spiritual guidance. But if we meditate on Scripture verses we commit to memory, we'll also receive divine guidance throughout the day. When we hear the Word preached to us, we may also confirm what God has spoken to us individually.

When we have a wealth of Scripture verses committed to memory, the Holy Spirit will have a multitude of medications prepared for us during times of crisis. Matthew quotes Jesus to this effect: "When they hand you over, do not worry about how you are to speak or what you are to say; for what you are to say will be given to you at that time; for it is not you who speak, but the Spirit of your Father speaking through you" (Matthew 10:19-20).

At times the Spirit helps us recall the verses we've memorized; Jesus reminds us of this in the Gospel of John. "The Advocate, the Holy Spirit, whom the Father will send in my name, will teach you everything, and remind you of all that I have said to you" (John 14:26).

Keep in mind Psalm 119 as you commit yourself to the wonderful privilege of divine guidance granted to all those who love him. "Great peace have those who love your law; / nothing can make them stumble" (v. 165).

PRACTICE

Memorize for Recollection

Memorization is easier when we use mnemonic principles that assist our remembering process. Architect R. Buckminster Fuller reminds us, "Everyone is born a genius, but the process of living de-geniuses them" (quoted in *Color Outside the Lines* by Howard G. Hendricks). If everyone is born a genius, what we need is not a better brain; we need to learn how to use what God has given us.

Our capacity to recall depends on our method of committing data to memory. There are at least three levels of memory.

The first level is *registration*, where we receive information. This involves making conscious sense of data as they enter us. It's more than simply allowing information to come in; we judge, sort and approve the data for long-term memory.

The second level is *retention*. This is the actual process of "writing" the data on our mind for long-term memory.

The third level is *recall*. This is the process of retrieving data from the memory file. It requires the skill of imaging and relating the data with a particular situation. This involves reflection in a systematic way. If we end up saying, "I just can't recall the verse no matter how much I try," our attempt to memorize wasn't systematic enough.

A systematic, three-dimensional way of memorizing Scripture accomplishes what sheer will alone can't.

This is why it's important to think about recall at the time we commit something to memory. What we're able to commit to memory with the utmost speed doesn't necessarily stay memorized for long. Dramatic content is unforgettable.

Emotion and memory. We remember things that have a major emotional effect on us—important emotional expressions like joy, grief, shock and fear.

Using the five senses. Most of what we retain in our memory has had a major impact on our minds. Here, our five senses come into play. If the Scripture passage we're trying to memorize is connected to more than one sense, it's much easier to remember. Leonardo da Vinci said that the five senses rule the soul of a person.

For the sake of memorizing Scripture, we need to develop our five senses. If we can see, hear, touch, taste and smell the Scriptures we're memorizing, we can more easily commit them to memory.

Jesus as teacher. When we read the Gospel narratives, we realize how effectively the Lord Jesus used the five senses in his teaching ministry. We notice that each parable interweaves memorable events, characters, life situations, sounds and colorful imagery.

Consider the events recorded in the Gospels: Jesus' baptism by John, his temptation in the wilderness, the Sermon on the Mount, the wedding at Cana, the feeding with five loaves and two fish, the meeting at the Mount of Transfiguration, the raising of Lazarus, the prayer at Gethsemane, the crucifixion, and the resurrection. Jesus applied effective mnemonic principles in his teaching and in bringing us the Word.

The biblical authors used easy-to-remember and earthy images: lambs, garments of skin, rocks, shepherds, blood, white garments, vines, figs, the tabernacle and temple are all images that are easy to recall.

Use imaginative power. Imaginative power is important for memorization; some people call it the sixth sense because it is such an effective learning tool. Imagination helps form a picture in our mind, which helps us retain the memory. Thus using our imagination when memorizing Scripture will speed up the process.

Repetition sharpens the memory. Don't hesitate to review or get weary of reviewing memorized Scripture. Repeatedly reviewing the words is like sharpening a dull blade. The more we sharpen our memory, the easier it becomes to memorize.

If the ax is dull
  and its edge unsharpened,
more strength is needed
  but skill will bring success. (Ecclesiastes 10:10 NIV)

29

BECOMING GOD'S INSTRUMENT

Let the word of Christ dwell in you richly;
teach and admonish one another in all wisdom;
and with gratitude in your hearts
sing psalms, hymns, and spiritual songs to God.

COLOSSIANS 3:16

God loves us. He wants all who have come to faith in Christ to participate in the joy of building his kingdom. Alas, not every Christian accepts the invitation. This isn't God's fault. But if we do accept God's invitation, we must work to be worthy of it. Only then will we begin to bear fruit in ministry.

Naturally, when such an invitation comes, not everyone recognizes it for what it is; only those spiritually prepared can respond accordingly. Memorizing Scripture helps; it get us on the invitation list.

Not all who respond get invited to the same party. Paul describes the varieties of instruments God uses: "In a large house there are utensils not only of gold and silver but also of wood and clay, some for special use, some for ordinary" (2 Timothy 2:20).

Cleansing from sin. The Word of God exposes sin, cleanses us from sin and sanctifies us. Jesus said to the apostles, "You have already been cleansed by the word that I have spoken to you" (John 15:3). And Jesus interceded for the apostles to the Father: "Sanctify them in the truth; your word is truth" (John 17:17).

When the Word abides in us, we may be cleansed and set apart as his special instrument. Hold fast to the Word with your heart, and the Word will take hold of you.

We read of the tragic cases in which those who despised his Word were abandoned by God. For example, Samuel said to King Saul, "Because you have rejected the word of the LORD, / he has also rejected you from being king" (1 Samuel 15:23).

On the other hand, God used the apostles as special instruments when they were holding fast to the Word for dear life; Luke noted, "The twelve called together the whole community of the disciples and said, 'It is not right that we should neglect the word of God in order to wait on tables' " (Acts 6:2).

When we let the Word of God dwell in us richly, we experience the powerful presence of the Holy Spirit; the Word and the Spirit go hand in hand. As Jesus said, "He whom God has sent speaks the words of God, for he gives the Spirit without measure" (John 3:34). He also said, "It is the spirit that gives life; the flesh is useless. The words that I have spoken to you are spirit and life" (John 6:63).

Because the Word and the Spirit are interdependent, wisdom follows the abundance of God's Word. This is true not only because wisdom is found in the Word but also because the Holy Spirit is called the Spirit of wisdom. The prophet Isaiah put it this way. "The spirit of the LORD shall rest on him, / the spirit of wisdom and understanding, / the spirit of counsel and might, / the spirit of knowledge and the fear of the LORD" (Isaiah 11:2).

This is concretely exemplified in Colossians: "Let the word of Christ dwell in you richly; teach and admonish one another in all wisdom; and with gratitude in your hearts sing psalms, hymns, and spiritual songs to God" (Colossians 3:16).

Nothing is more essential for the minister of the gospel than spiritual training. Nothing is more essential to spiritual training than memorizing Scripture.

PRACTICE

Aim for Mastery

In order to become skilled in serving the Lord, we must train ourselves to be fully skilled in the Word of God: "Hezekiah spoke encouragingly to all the Levites who showed good skill in the service of the LORD. So the people ate the food of the festival for seven days, sacrificing offerings of well-being and giving thanks to the LORD the God of their ancestors" (2 Chronicles 30:22).

Relating parts to the whole. Becoming skillful with the Word involves connecting and relating memorized Scripture with Jesus, who is the Lord of Scripture (John 5:39). It's relating Christ to various major themes of the Bible, such as knowing God, imitating God, obeying the will of God, the names of God, the kingdom of God, the glory of God, the gospel, the message of the cross, the blood of the Lamb, the living water of the Spirit, the power of the Word.

Becoming skillful with the Word entails memorizing verses and seeing the interrelationship of practical themes such as fearing God, love, eternal life, prayer, fellowship, evangelism, discipleship, wisdom, obedience, holiness, gentleness, self-control, spiritual gifts, fruit, grace, thanksgiving, commitment, guidance, promise, heart and covenant. The important thing to remember is that we must begin small, memorize thoroughly and relate newly memorized verses to the rest of our knowledge of Scripture.

Seeing relationships gives rise to synergy. Preserving, accumulating and using the material effectively depends on reflection and seeing meaningful connections. Tony Buzan, educational consultant and author of *How to Mind Map,* teaches that we learn best by association. He coaches people to link new things to what they already know for effective learning and memorization.

When we memorize and reflect on the Word through repetition, different scriptural passages come together and synergism occurs. This is another reason we need to repeatedly reflect on the concepts learned through cross-referencing. If we retain what we've learned, learning new concepts and insights becomes easier and more effective. This is the path to becoming truly skilled in the knowledge of the Bible.

A broken bucket in the time of need. I often review the passages I use most. I can't take them for granted. I remind myself with the proverb, "Even a broken bucket is hard to find in the time of need."

Indeed, we should begin with those verses familiar to an average Christian. Whenever possible, begin with those that are simple, gradually progressing toward deeper truths. It's important to see logical and systematic coherence and the interrelationships between the Testaments as well as between the Gospels and the Epistles.

Relate the passages and relate them again. When you're relating two passages, use such tools as comparison and contrast, cause and effect, problem and solution, and progressive revelation. Comparing and contrasting passages can yield a more comprehensive and deeper understanding. This process can be applied in our study of biblical characters, events and places.

We can memorize passages that propose a problem and others that provide a solution. We'll encounter places where Scripture identifies the major problems of humanity, such as sin, salvation, suffering, sickness, poverty, success and failure, weakness, anxiety, fear, doubt, depression, relational conflicts, restoration, complacency, lust, and Satan.

Memorizing Scripture by heart takes a lifetime. Reflection and seeing relationships are scientific and spiritual. This gradual process continues throughout a lifetime, as if we were climbing a mountain that surprises us with breathtaking sights at various intervals. Memorizing with the goal of becoming truly skillful with the Bible helps us to see deeper, higher and mysterious dimensions of the spiritual life.

As the Scriptures gradually become related to our memory, repetition adds to an interpretive pattern of thought. This habit of mind recognizes that more things are lost than retained; however, we need not become anxious, for our brain adjusts itself and develops as we use it more.

Let the mind breathe. Our brain is more often underused than overused. Either way we're responsible for using it wisely by giving it appropriate rest. Time to pause, reflect and meditatively pray provide fitting and refreshing rest to our mind.

Listening to music, walking in the park, breathing deeply and laughing are all excellent ways to allow our mind to "breathe." Of course, we need to come back into focus when we're looking for a solution to a problem. However, we can embrace a detached attitude when we do so. We may also experience times of enlightenment and illumination during problem-solving; often this happens after we let go of the issue for a while or after a good night's rest.

When we become too immersed in or occupied with a problem, we tend to lose clarity of judgment; that's the time to take a break. I take regular breaks to restore my judgment and creativity. Times of reflection and solitude also help.

Another helpful tip comes from the use of our brain activity. The left side of our brain predominantly engages in language, logic, numbers, continuity, examining details, symbolic expressions and judgments. The right side occupies itself with areas that concern image, rhythm, music, imagination, color, overview, pattern and emotion. Creativity requires that the two work together. Harnessing the brain in this fashion leads to more effective understanding in general and memorization of the Word in particular.

The surplus principle. When our knowledge is abundant in one area, insights can emerge immediately and rather surprisingly; things seem to fall into place in an orderly fashion. Like a reservoir that collects water until it overflows, a surplus of knowledge on one topic overflows into other areas.

When we let the Word dwell in us richly, we become like a well, always able to refresh others on demand. This happens quite often when we memorize Scripture, study the Bible, or prepare a sermon or lecture. The more we share the Word, the more we're replenished. The more we're replenished, the more we use the Word to bless and love others.

With faithful heart and skillful hands. When David was anointed by God to be a shepherd to Israel, he led the people faithfully: "With upright heart he tended them, / and guided them with skillful hand" (Psalm 78:72). Our commitment to memorize Scripture has the same effect; it keeps our hearts faithful and our memories are handled skillfully.

30

FULFILLING
YOUR MISSION

This book of the law shall not depart out of your mouth;
you shall meditate on it day and night,
so that you may be careful to act in accordance
with all that is written in it.
For then you shall make your way prosperous,
and then you shall be successful.

JOSHUA 1:8

According to the principles laid out in Scripture, God's people ought to succeed in life. Please note, when the Bible uses the word *success*, it refers to accomplishing something God has entrusted to us.

David prayed that Solomon would be successful: "Now, my son, the LORD be with you, so that you may succeed in building the house of the LORD your God, as he has spoken concerning you" (1 Chronicles 22:11).

Nehemiah too prayed for success as he rebuilt the broken walls of Jerusalem. "O Lord, let your ear be attentive to the prayer of your servant, and to the prayer of your servants who delight in revering your name. Give success to your servant today, and grant him mercy in the sight of this man" (Nehemiah 1:11).

Biblical success means much more than prosperity. It includes developing God-given talents and accomplishing God-given tasks. This includes meditating on the Scripture already committed to memory.

Joshua encourages this sort of meditation: "This book of the law shall not depart out of your mouth; you shall meditate on it day and night, so that you may be careful to act in accordance with all that is written in it. For then you shall make your way prosperous, and then you shall be successful" (Joshua 1:8).

All success begins in the mind. As the American poet Ralph Waldo Emerson observed, "thinking is the key" to work done well. Thought is the seed that will eventually bear fruit. Seed falling on the good ground of the heart will create a positive future; it will create circumstances and events we can grow in. Scripture already committed to memory will contribute to further memorization of more Scripture.

For a person to become a success, God has to be present in him or her. Joseph is a wonderful example: "The LORD was with Joseph, and he became a successful man" (Genesis 39:2). The same is true of Joshua: "So the LORD was with Joshua; and his fame was in all the land" (Joshua 6:27).

How is God present with us? According to Scripture, it is through his Word. Walking with God can't begin without abiding in his Word.

Committing ourselves to holding his Word in our heart will help us keep stride with him.

PRACTICE

When Memorization Bogs Down

When memorization bogs down or turns sour, as it surely will, the tendency is to stop the process altogether. Instead, it is better to spend the time you allotted for memorization in some spiritual refreshment, like checking your inner dispositions about the whole project.

A proper attitude is more important than the techniques used in memorizing Scripture. It's critical that we are well disposed toward the goal in general and are willing to commit the hard hours to do the work.

Since success in life is based not on *what* we see but *how* we see, our greatest stumbling block lies within ourselves. As Jan Christian Smuts, a prominent South African statesman, said, "A man is not defeated by his opponents but by himself."

A positive spirit is our first principle in all our inner struggles. Even a quiet, humdrum, ordinary life has its challenges, if only competing with ourself. As British artist Stewart Johnson has rightly said, "Our business in life is not to get ahead of others, but ahead of ourselves—to break our own records, to outstrip our yesterday by our today."

The following are a dozen inner dispositions against which we can check our own heart.

*A **loving heart**.* Love is the starting point for memorizing Scripture. Love shows concern, willingness to invest hard time and a certain hilarity: "Their delight is in the law of the LORD, / and on his law they meditate day and night" (Psalm 1:2).

The object of our love is Scripture. The more we memorize it, the closer we come to it, the easier we understand it, the surer we remember it and impress it on our hearts.

Love and learning have always been relative to each other. We memorize Scripture to love God—we love God by memorizing Scripture.

Remember Israel's "charter of education": "You shall love the LORD your God with all your heart, and with all your soul, and with all your might. Keep these words that I am commanding you today in your heart" (Deuteronomy 6:5-6).

The apostles and disciples loved Jesus; that's why they preserved his words and actions. In Scripture, with our inner eye we can see Jesus and with our inner ear we can hear him. Memorizing Scripture does that, and it increases our love for him.

The intensity of our love for God will carry over into every other area of learning.

A reverent heart. To fear God is the highest form of knowledge and wisdom. "The fear of the LORD is the beginning of knowledge; / fools despise wisdom and instruction" (Proverbs 1:7). And "the fear of the LORD is the beginning of wisdom, / and the knowledge of the Holy One is insight" (Proverbs 9:10).

Fear of God is a major theme in the Bible. Isaiah saw its fulfillment.

The Spirit of the LORD shall rest on him,
    the spirit of wisdom and understanding,
    the spirit of counsel and might,
    the spirit of knowledge and the fear of the LORD.
His delight shall be in the fear of the LORD.

He shall not judge by what his eyes see,
    or decide by what his ears hear. (Isaiah 11:2-3)

Our Lord's great concern is to implant in us a heart that reveres him.

Jeremiah tells us much the same thing.

> I will give them one heart and one way, that they may fear me for all time, for their own good and the good of their children after them. I will make an everlasting covenant with them, never to draw back from doing good to them; and I will put the fear of me in their hearts, so that they may not turn from me. (Jeremiah 32:39-40)

The heart that fears God is ripe for blessing, according to Jeremiah. "I will rejoice in doing good to them, and I will plant them in this land in faithfulness, with all my heart and all my soul" (Jeremiah 32:41).

God looks favorably on those who memorize his Word; he considers their commitment an expression of reverence for him. But he brings trouble to those who don't respect his Word: "Those who despise the word bring destruction on themselves, / but those who respect the commandment will be rewarded" (Proverbs 13:13).

God even abandons the troubled. Samuel, for example, rebukes Saul: "Rebellion is no less a sin than divination, / and stubbornness is like iniquity and idolatry. / Because you have rejected the word of the LORD, / he has also rejected you from being king" (1 Samuel 15:23).

According to the psalmist, God paves the way for those who love his Word: "Great peace have those who love your law; / nothing can make them stumble" (Psalm 119:165).

According to Isaiah, fearing God is a treasure itself.

> He will be the stability of your times,
> abundance of salvation, wisdom, and knowledge;
> the fear of the LORD is Zion's treasure. (Isaiah 33:6)

Fearing God doesn't mean being frightened by him; it means loving and considering him as precious, esteeming him as the highest priority. Let's follow David's example in fearing God and teach others the same through memorizing Scripture.

> O fear the LORD, you his holy ones,
>> for those who fear him have no want.
> The young lions suffer want and hunger,
>> but those who seek the LORD lack no good thing.

> Come, O children, listen to me;
>> I will teach you the fear of the LORD. (Psalm 34:9-11)

A heart set on Jesus. The third inner disposition in memorizing Scripture has to do with impressing our minds with the Lord Jesus Christ. We do this so our knowledge of Christ will cause him to be honored in our being.

The apostle Paul's only aim was Jesus Christ:

> Whatever gains I had, these I have come to regard as loss because of Christ. More than that, I regard everything as loss because of the surpassing value of knowing Christ Jesus my Lord. For his sake I have suffered the loss of all things, and I regard them as rubbish, in order that I may gain Christ and be found in him, not having a righteousness of my own that comes from the law, but one that comes through faith in Christ, the righteousness from God based on faith. (Philippians 3:7-9)

In the same letter the apostle makes a bold confession. "It is my eager expectation and hope that I will not be put to shame in any way, but that by my speaking with all boldness, Christ will be exalted now as always in my body, whether by life or by death. For to me, living is Christ and dying is gain" (Philippians 1:20-21).

Receiving the Word of God is tantamount to welcoming Jesus into our heart. In the same way, memorizing the Word, letting the Word dwell in us, implies we're being filled with the Spirit of Jesus.

Knowing Christ deeply can't begin without his Word dwelling in our hearts richly.

A trusting heart. Memorizing Scripture is a ministry of the Holy

Spirit. When we wish to discern the meaning of words memorized, we depend on the Holy Spirit. Paul discerned this: "These things God has revealed to us through the Spirit; for the Spirit searches everything, even the depths of God" (1 Corinthians 2:10). Paul continues the thought several verses later: "We speak of these things in words not taught by human wisdom but taught by the Spirit, interpreting spiritual things to those who are spiritual" (v. 13).

What might and power can't accomplish, the Spirit can: "This is the word of the LORD to Zerubbabel: Not by might, nor by power, but by my spirit, says the LORD of hosts" (Zechariah 4:6).

The Spirit gives us the patience to fit memorization into our lifestyle. Paul describes this: "I pray that, according to the riches of his glory, he may grant that you may be strengthened in your inner being with power through his Spirit" (Ephesians 3:16). In addition to being patient, we must pray.

The Spirit helps us recall those passages we've learned by heart. According to Jesus, "The Advocate, the Holy Spirit, whom the Father will send in my name, will teach you everything, and remind you of all that I have said to you" (John 14:26).

A faithful heart. The fifth inner disposition in memorizing Scripture is a faithful heart.

Memorization must be habitual; we must be faithful. We lay one brick at a time, memorize one word at a time. We must show up every day; it's the job of a lifetime. Though recall of words just memorized is difficult at the beginning, it becomes easier with time.

Regularity will teach us methods and skills. Faithfulness will reveal the sweetness of the Word. Repetition will turn us into experts.

A faithful heart belongs to God, and God responds to it. The psalmist puts it this way: "Trust in the LORD, and do good; / so you will live in the land, and enjoy security" (Psalm 37:3).

A faithful heart means being faithful in little things, considering them precious; it also means not easily giving them up, finishing them off well.

Determining the right direction is much more important than

calculating the time of arrival at a goal. Once started in the right direction and no matter what the traveling conditions are, I must finish the race.

Daniel is a good model of perseverance: "Although Daniel knew that the document had been signed, he continued to go to his house, which had windows in its upper room open toward Jerusalem, and to get down on his knees three times a day to pray to his God and praise him, just as he had done previously" (Daniel 6:10). Hosea ascribes this persevering character to our God:

> Let us know, let us press on to know the LORD;
>   his appearing is as sure as the dawn;
> he will come to us like the showers,
>   like the spring rains that water the earth. (Hosea 6:3)

A faithful person doesn't despair or give up in the face of failures. Instead he or she presses on, refuses discouragement, completes the marathon; at the end comes the inevitable smile of victory. This is the secret behind all faithful people who attain their goal.

Faithfulness is obedience to God's command. That's why we cannot fear or fret. Faithfulness, in fact, is a fruit of the Spirit (Galatians 5:22). Thus, it is not what we produce, but what we bear. It is Scripture memorization that enables us to bear the fruit of faithfulness, and also enables us to keep our pace, not being affected by the circumstances whether they are good or bad.

When memorizing Scripture, I'm often reminded of the saying "faithfulness knows no end."

A pure heart. A pure heart meditates on the Word of God. A clean heart embraces the Scripture verses. Immoral thoughts just muddy up the process.

Jesus had something to say about immoral words. "What comes out of the mouth proceeds from the heart, and this is what defiles" (Matthew 15:18). Unclean words snuff the Spirit.

Instead, according to Paul, "Let no evil talk come out of your mouths, but only what is useful for building up, as there is need, so that your words may give grace to those who hear" (Ephesians 4:29).

Satan afflicts our minds and souls; he suggests lustful and boastful thoughts. At such times we must immediately repent, purify our minds and hearts.

Each time I memorize the Word, I find it a trudge. My dark side sheds crocodile tears and breaks up my comfort level. But when I bring these carnal thoughts before God in repentance, a divine sweetness fills my soul.

Memorizing his Word is a spiritual activity; it generates a spiritually motivated work of the mind. That leaves no room for carnal thoughts. Paul says much the same thing:

> Those who live according to the flesh set their minds on the things of the flesh, but those who live according to the Spirit set their minds on the things of the Spirit. To set the mind on the flesh is death, but to set the mind on the Spirit is life and peace. For this reason the mind that is set on the flesh is hostile to God; it does not submit to God's law—indeed it cannot, and those who are in the flesh cannot please God. (Romans 8:5-8)

In order to have victory over temptation, we shouldn't just fight carnal thoughts; we should reinforce our spiritual thoughts; we should memorize the Word of God.

When we walk in the Spirit of light, we dispel the fog of darkness.

A humble heart. Abraham Lincoln, we are told, was someone who learned from others, no matter what their profession. He considered each chance encounter another teachable moment. "I will prepare myself and someday my chance will come." Perhaps this kind of humility was one of the factors that made him a great leader.

On the one hand, the humble heart holds an opinion tentatively until it is tested by time. On the other hand, it enjoys the incomplete state of things and remains flexible.

Mistakes and failures are part of the learning process. Albert Einstein once said, "Anyone who has never made a mistake has never tried anything new."

When we make mistakes or when our performance is poor, we shouldn't label them as failures; rather, we should consider them searches for a better plan of action. Having an open mind simply means that we're evaluating our options.

We mustn't become enslaved by past failures. Some of us may have a negative attitude about memorizing Scripture; perhaps we've been ridiculed by those who have a better memory than we do. Others may say that they've tried it before, but it's too difficult.

It's worthwhile to set aside this conclusion for a moment and honestly ask a question. "Did I really put in the effort? Did I really give myself a fair chance?"

Still others had the desire, but didn't know how to go about it. I suggest that you show this book to them.

A final word from Peter. "All of you must clothe yourselves with humility in your dealings with one another, for 'God opposes the proud, / but gives grace to the humble' " (1 Peter 5:5). Peter was quoting from Proverbs 3:34.

A wise heart. *Bad* is working wisely but lazily. *Worse* is working sincerely but foolishly. *Worst* is working hard but tragically. The end of the book of Judges is a case in point. "In those days there was no king in Israel; all the people did what was right in their own eyes" (Judges 21:25). That is to say, they lived without any standards or values.

Paul said as much about the Gentiles. "I can testify that they have a zeal for God, but it is not enlightened" (Romans 10:2). Passion, if it's to be allowed, must be accompanied by knowledge.

Certain principles play a role in the process of memorizing Scripture. More important than our natural aptitude is the wise application of certain methods.

Certainly, we should seek God for wisdom. According to James, "If any of you is lacking in wisdom, ask God, who gives to all generously and ungrudgingly, and it will be given you" (James 1:5).

We should also benefit from others who have gained wisdom: "Whoever walks with the wise becomes wise, / but the companion of fools suffers harm" (Proverbs 13:20).

This will continue to sharpen our skills even further, according to Proverbs. "Iron sharpens iron, / and one person sharpens the wits of another" (Proverbs 27:17).

The ongoing fellowship of saints around the Word will encourage beginners to benefit from this value we place on memorizing Scripture.

Acquiring these wise skills in memorizing the Word requires great effort. This should come as no surprise.

Wisdom knows where and when to invest one's energy.

A believing heart. Confidence and assurance are indispensable in attaining victory. Our unlimited potential is part of the puzzle. We can summarize it in three ways.

First, God lives in us. God works in us through his grace by influencing our desires: "It is God who is at work in you, enabling you both to will and to work for his good pleasure" (Philippians 2:13). Further Paul exclaimed, "I can do all things through him who strengthens me" (Philippians 4:13).

Second, we possess the Word of God. God created the world with his Word. "In these last days he has spoken to us by a Son, whom he appointed heir of all things, through whom he also created the worlds" (Hebrews 1:2). And "by faith we understand that the worlds were prepared by the word of God, so that what is seen was made from things that are not visible" (Hebrews 11:3).

The author of Hebrews also says, "He is the reflection of God's glory and the exact imprint of God's very being, and he sustains all things by his powerful word. When he had made purification for sins, he sat down at the right hand of the Majesty on high" (Hebrews 1:3).

Third, we've been created in God's image, he commissioned us to have dominion over the world, and he endowed us with a capacity for eternity. Genesis puts it this way: "God blessed them, and God said to them, 'Be fruitful and multiply, and fill the earth and subdue it; and have dominion over the fish of the sea and over the birds of the air and over every living thing that moves upon the earth' " (Genesis 1:28).

Jesus also foresaw the potential entrusted to his own disciples, saying, "Very truly, I tell you, the one who believes in me will also do the works that I do and, in fact, will do greater works than these, because I am going to the Father" (John 14:12).

Most of the time our problem isn't our inability but our unwillingness. We're ready to give up before we begin. If we haven't started already, it's time to pick up the challenge. It's time to start memorizing the Word. We usually underestimate what has been given to us. Our mind is incredibly capable of learning new material and expressing it creatively.

Scott Thorpe, who wrote *How to Think Like Einstein,* observes that our minds are marvels. Our minds "have nearly unlimited capacity to create and conceive." He believes that we are "closer to genius than we think."

Memorizing Scripture and faith are interrelated. Faith relies on the imagination of what hasn't come to pass—"Faith is the assurance of things hoped for, the conviction of things not seen" (Hebrews 11:1)—and on the confession with our mouths.

When Abraham believed, he believed in God as one "who gives life to the dead and calls into existence the things that do not exist" (Romans 4:17).

A confession of faith strengthens our conviction and inflames our heart. When we memorize Scripture, we confess our faith and promise to use these words with vigor and forthrightness.

When God equips people for a mission, he also transforms their speech. When Jeremiah was summoned by God to be a prophet to the nations, he responded, "Ah, Lord God! Truly I do not know how to speak, for I am only a boy" (Jeremiah 1:6). Here, God instructs Jeremiah to drop the language of timidity and put the language of confidence in its place: "Do not say, 'I am only a boy'; / for you shall go to all to whom I send you, / and you shall speak whatever I command you" (v. 7).

God corrected Jeremiah; he wasn't a child but "a prophet to the nations. . . . And I for my part have made you today a fortified city, an iron pillar and a bronze wall" (Jeremiah 1:5, 18). In this way, he changed Jeremiah's self-concept, which in turn transformed his life.

Our confessions and endless dialogue with ourselves are as important as our prayers to God.

A whole heart. Without proper training, aggressive weapons are no weapons at all; all soldiers of the world know this. All the people of the world are soldiers, but in the spiritual battle against the enemy, they don't know this. They possess the most effective weapon, but they keep it in their arsenal; these spiritual soldiers don't know how to use it and hence are destined to lose. Which is another way of saying, having Bibles on our bookshelves won't help. We have to take them off the shelves and memorize the Scripture verses contained therein. If we do this, victory will certainly be ours.

It's a question of discipline, wrote Henri Nouwen in his *Making All Things New.* "A spiritual life without discipline is impossible. Discipline is the other side of discipleship. The practice of spiritual discipline makes us more sensitive to the small gentle voice of God."

When we apply ourselves wholeheartedly to the discipline of memorizing Scripture, there's a certain rigor, the grunt and grind of basic training. But eventually we emerge as highly trained soldiers ready for special operations of all sorts.

In *The Road Less Traveled* psychologist Scott Peck notes that discipline is "choosing some discomfort now in order to enjoy the pleasures later." Rather than viewing discipline as a plague to avoid, we must embrace it like a door to be opened.

The spiritual life is often compared to athletics. To attain excellence we've got to master the basics. To master the basics, we must train every day. If we forsake the basics, we'll lose our edge. And so it is with memorizing Scripture. Paul sets the matter straight: "Put these things into practice, devote yourself to them, so that all may see your progress" (1 Timothy 4:15).

An obedient heart. Memorizing the Word isn't an end in itself; it's a means of learning truth and living it.

Living the truth deepens our knowledge of the truth, but only if we can remember it, and remembrance takes practice. According to some experts we remember approximately 20 percent of what we read, 30 percent of what we hear, 40 percent of what we see, 50 percent of what we say, 60 percent of what we do, and 90 percent of what we see, hear, say and do. Yes, practice makes perfect.

According to the letter of James, the Word must be humbly received. If we don't put it into practice, we're just deceiving ourselves. Here's what James has to say on the subject in full.

> Rid yourselves of all sordidness and rank growth of wickedness, and welcome with meekness the implanted word that has the power to save your souls.
>
> But be doers of the word, and not merely hearers who deceive themselves. For if any are hearers of the word and not doers, they are like those who look at themselves in a mirror; for they look at themselves and, on going away, immediately forget what they were like. But those who look into the perfect law, the law of liberty, and persevere, being not hearers who forget but doers who act—they will be blessed in their doing. (James 1:21-25)

Living truth means obeying the Great Commission: "Go therefore and make disciples of all nations, baptizing them in the name of the Father and of the Son and of the Holy Spirit, and teaching them to obey everything that I have commanded you. And remember, I am with you always, to the end of the age" (Matthew 28:19-20).

A patient heart. Agriculture teaches us about the Father's heart. Jesus said, "I am the true vine, and my Father is the vinegrower" (John 15:1). He also used other farming imagery to teach about the kingdom of heaven; the parables of the soil and of the mustard seed come to mind.

Farmers believe in the incredible potential of a seed. They envision a great reality coming from something small. A leaf, a flower, a fruit, an orchard. Truly, farmers are dreamers, persons of vision and patience. So are those who memorize just one verse of Scripture.

When the weather allows, the farmer is rewarded with the fruit of the season. Jesus puts it this way: "The earth produces of itself, first the stalk, then the head, then the full grain in the head" (Mark 4:28). This same maturation process is also necessary before memorized Scripture can bear fruit in our lives.

Nothing acquired easily gives much satisfaction. Hence, I've always appreciated two verses from Psalm 126:

> May those who sow in tears
> reap with shouts of joy.
> Those who go out weeping,
> bearing the seed for sowing,
> shall come home with shouts of joy,
> carrying their sheaves. (vv. 5-6)

When we memorize the Word with the farmer's tears, sweat and love, we'll surely reap a great harvest. But note that the final joy is determined not by brains or talents, but by patience. Patience is always a prelude to perfection.

The letter of James teaches wisdom about change and maturity; he repeatedly insists on patience: "My brothers and sisters, whenever you face trials of any kind, consider it nothing but joy, because you know that the testing of your faith produces endurance; and let endurance have its full effect, so that you may be mature and complete, lacking in nothing" (James 1:2-4). As examples, James sets forth a farmer, a prophet and Job from the Old Testament; in each of these he stresses patience.

> Be patient, therefore, beloved, until the coming of the Lord. The farmer waits for the precious crop from the earth, being patient with it until it receives the early and the late rains. You also must be patient. Strengthen your hearts, for the coming of the Lord is near. (James 5:7-8)

Learning Scripture by heart happens only through patience; a genius can't make it happen any sooner; perhaps someone with a photographic memory can.

By the way, a genius is merely a person who refuses to give up, who accomplishes what he or she has set out to do. Inventor Thomas Edison would buy that: "Being a genius is being tenacious."

With regard to memorizing Scripture, don't back off from what you've set out to do.

Remember the old adage "Patience is bitter, but its fruit is sweet."

CONCLUSION

Meditating on Psalm 1

I meditated on Psalm 1 recently. I chose this psalm because it speaks directly to Scripture memorization and meditation. I'd like to share some of the fruits I received. (The English-language Scripture citations in this meditation have been taken from the New American Standard Bible.)

PSALM 1

> ¹How blessed is the man who does not walk in the counsel
>   of the wicked,
>   Nor stand in the path of sinners,
>   Nor sit in the seat of scoffers!
> ²But his delight is in the law of the LORD,
>   And in His law he meditates day and night.
> ³He will be like a tree firmly planted by streams of water,
>   Which yields its fruit in its season
>   And its leaf does not wither;
>   And in whatever he does, he prospers.
> ⁴The wicked are not so,
>   But they are like chaff which the wind drives away.
> ⁵Therefore the wicked will not stand in the judgment,
>   Nor sinners in the assembly of the righteous.
> ⁶For the LORD knows the way of the righteous,
>   But the way of the wicked will perish.

THE BLESSED PERSON

Job, Psalms, Proverbs, Ecclesiastes and Song of Songs are the wisdom books of the Old Testament. Psalm 1 is the key that opens all the doors of wisdom. Understanding Psalm 1 leads to understanding all wisdom. When we memorize Psalm 1 we encounter heavenly delights.

Verse 1 begins with "blessed is the man." God wants us to be blessed. He doesn't want us to pursue blessing; he wants us to become blessed. He doesn't want us to enjoy blessedness for a time; he wants us to experience blessing for a lifetime.

The blessed one in verse 1 is related to the last part of verse 3. "In whatever he does, he prospers" tells us that a blessed person becomes prosperous in the end. Prosperity follows him or her like a faithful dog.

True blessing is in being sufficient. A blessed person is one who transcends all circumstances and conditions; the blessed one is simply sufficient in being who he or she is, and shares this blessing from God with others.

The Old Testament patriarch Joseph received the blessing of prosperity: "The LORD was with Joseph, so he became a successful man. And he was in the house of his master, the Egyptian. Now his master saw that the LORD was with him and how the LORD caused all that he did to prosper in his hand" (Genesis 39:2-3). Joseph prospered because God was with him. True prosperity resides in walking with God.

To become prosperous doesn't mean we're free from trouble. It means we prospered despite troubles. Joseph didn't pursue prosperity when he was living as a slave and a prisoner, or when he was serving as the governor, but he was prosperous nonetheless. Wherever he went he drew prosperity unto himself and shared it with others. And we should do the same.

A preacher shouldn't seek to wow a congregation; rather, the preacher should labor to become a spiritual person. A preacher may labor for a hundred hours preparing a sermon, but if he or she's a spiritual person, spiritual words will flow without effort.

Jesus was a spiritual person; whatever he spoke was truly spiritual.

The famous Sermon on the Mount wasn't the result of elaborate preparation; we're told that he just opened his mouth and taught.

How then can we become blessed and therefore sufficiently spiritual persons? What's the lesson we need to grasp from Psalm 1? What would you say is this person's distinctive character trait?

TRAITS OF THE BLESSED PERSON

A blessed person is a wise person who is able to discern many things.

A wise person knows good people from bad. Verse 1 tells us we must be on guard against the wicked, sinners and scoffers. In verses 5-6 we encounter the righteous person, the sort of person we should walk with. We should avoid those who aren't righteous. This is wisdom.

Divine opportunities come through our encounters with others; these are often venues of blessing from God. But not all encounters are good; tragedies have struck some because they couldn't tell a good from a bad friend. We must avoid the bad and build relationships with the good.

A wise person distinguishes godly and worldly wisdom. Verse 1 says the blessed person avoids "the counsel of the wicked." Worldly wisdom is devilish, makes bread with stones, skips the proper process and wants success on demand; it's preoccupied with instant profits. Worldly wisdom is always impatient; it flowers early, then wilts forever. It is full of evil things, for worldly wisdom is filled with lies generated by the devil, the father of lies. That's why Jesus makes this explicit: "You are of your father the devil, and you want to do the desires of your father. He was a murderer from the beginning, and does not stand in the truth because there is no truth in him. Wherever he speaks a lie, he speaks from his own nature, for he is a liar and the father of lies" (John 8:44).

On the other hand, godly wisdom is vertical; it comes from heaven above. Because it is vertical, it has an overview. It is not shortsighted. It is always patient and, in that way, reflects God's own divine nature. It seems small in the beginning, but it will be slowly prosperous. Godly wisdom is like a seed in a farmer's hand.

Moreover, the wisdom from above is a pure one. It is written in James 3:17, "But the wisdom that comes from heaven is first of all pure; then peace-loving, considerate, submissive, full of mercy and good fruit, impartial and sincere" (NIV).

A wise person knows which path to walk. In verse 6 the wicked will come to ruin. "The LORD knows the way of the righteous, / But the way of the wicked will perish." The path of the righteous is narrow, difficult, straight and has no detours. On the other hand, the way of the wicked is broad, easy and is full of detours.

Jesus exhorts us to walk the narrow path: "Enter through the narrow gate; for the gate is wide and the way is broad that leads to destruction, and there are many who enter through it. For the gate is small and the way is narrow that leads to life, and there are few who find it" (Matthew 7:13-14).

Having too many roads to choose from can get a person lost. The not-so-righteous person would pick the shorter, more picturesque and smooth route through the woods. But the righteous person would choose the difficult and longer route; in the long run it's more secure because it basks in the light of the Lord.

This is confirmed in Proverbs:

> The path of the righteous is like the light of dawn,
> That shines brighter and brighter until the full day.
> The way of the wicked is like darkness;
> They do not know over what they stumble. (Proverbs 4:18-19)

A wise person knows when to sit and when to stand. God hates the person who doesn't know his or her station or manners. Satan, also known as Lucifer, coveted God's position and crowded him when he sat or stood; for that he was thrown out of heaven. A truly wise person knows his or her station and manners.

A blessed person also meditates on the Word of God. When we are blessed, we have wisdom. Wise people know that they must cling to the most important thing—and they know how to hold fast to its essence. Blessed persons cling to and delight in the Word of God.

Let's look at verse 2. "His delight is in the law of the LORD, / And in His law he meditates day and night."

"His delight is in the law of the LORD" means that he loves the Word of God. Since love is conveyed through concern, this verse expresses his concern for Scripture. He considers it precious, reveres it with his heart.

To revere God's Word means to revere God himself. Here we encounter the core wisdom in Proverbs:

> The fear of the LORD is the beginning of knowledge;
>> Fools despise wisdom and instruction. (Proverbs 1:7)

> The fear of the LORD is the beginning of wisdom,
>> And the knowledge of the Holy One is understanding.
> (Proverbs 9:10)

Revering God is one of the key concepts of Scripture.

> The Spirit of the LORD will rest on him,
>> The spirit of wisdom and understanding,
>> The spirit of counsel and strength,
>> The spirit of knowledge and the fear of the LORD. (Isaiah 11:2)

Isaiah spoke of the coming Messiah who, after being anointed by the Holy Spirit, will rejoice in revering God the Father: "He will delight in the fear of the LORD" (Isaiah 11:3)

God blesses those who revere him. In fact, God promises a great blessing:

> How great is Your goodness,
>> Which You have stored up for those who fear You,
> Which You have wrought for those who take refuge in You,
>> Before the sons of men! (Psalm 31:19)

David confessed that one who reveres God will lack nothing.
> O fear the LORD, you His saints,
>> For to those who fear Him there is no want.
> The young lions do lack and suffer hunger;
>> But they who seek the LORD shall not be in want of any
>> good thing. (Psalm 34:9-10)

One of my favorite Scripture passages comes from Proverbs. "The reward of humility and the fear of the LORD / Are riches, honor and life" (Proverbs 22:4). God's amazing blessing is based on humility and revering of God. Wealth, glory and life await those who revere God; the root of this blessing is in meditating on his Word. God despises those who despise his Word, and gives reward to those who revere it.

"The one who despises the word will be in debt to it, / But the one who fears the commandment will be rewarded" (Proverbs 13:13). A person who meditates and loves God's Word will enjoy great peace. He or she encounters no hindrances: "Those who love your law have great peace, / And nothing causes them to stumble" (Psalm 119:165). A person who meditates on his Word is truly blessed.

A wise person is blessed with fruitfulness. Verse 3 tells us the blessed person is "like a tree firmly planted by streams of water,"

> Which yields its fruit in its season
> And its leaf does not wither;
> And in whatever he does, he prospers.

"Yields its fruit in its season" means that this person isn't in a hurry, not seeking quick success; he or she respects the process. Fruits give their full flavor when they're harvested at the end of the season. Likewise, the person who meditates on the Word will eventually give spiritual flavor, beauty and fragrance.

"Yields its fruit in its season" also tells us that the root is deep enough, stretched well into the soil, watered by streams of water. "Streams of water" symbolize God himself, for Jeremiah 17:13 tells us that God is the source of living water.

A person who's rooted in God has branches heavy with fruit. Joseph was such a person:

> Joseph is a fruitful bough,
> A fruitful bough by a spring;
> Its branches run over a wall. (Genesis 49:22)

A person rooted in God need fear nothing; he or she is like a tree planted by the streams of water. Jeremiah says this about this tree:

> For he will be like a tree planted by the water,
>> That extends its roots by a stream
> And will not fear when the heat comes;
>> But its leaves will be green,
>> And it will not be anxious in a year of drought
>> Nor cease to yield fruit. (Jeremiah 17:8)

People rooted in God are unwavering. Even in the year of drought, they don't stop bearing fruit; they're steadfast, full of peace and unaffected by circumstances. "The steadfast of mind You will keep in perfect peace, / Because he trusts in you" (Isaiah 26:3).

This person rooted deeply by the streams of water knows how to keep silent. He or she shows depth of character when speaking or remaining silent. But "the wicked are not so, / . . . they are like chaff which the wind drives away" (Psalm 1:4).

The psalmist is using picturesque language of contrast; he distinguishes between the righteous fruitful tree and the wicked chaff blowing in the wind. A person who's like chaff lacks substance. This is because he or she lacks meditation, the depth of thought.

A wise person is blessed with evergreen leaves. Verse 3 tells us that "its leaf does not wither." This points to a manifestation of beauty and health. Let's read that passage from Jeremiah again.

> For he will be like a tree planted by the water,
>> That extends its roots by a stream
> And will not fear when the heat comes;
>> But its leaves will be green,
>> And it will not be anxious in a year of drought
>> Nor cease to yield fruit. (Jeremiah 17:8)

The tree planted by a stream will show vigor even with the coming heat wave. We notice that people who meditate on the Word day and night have a gleam about them. It's as if they live with unending youth. They overcome life's anxieties by the power of the Word. The gloom of life's worries dries up the bones: "A joyful heart is good medicine, / But a broken spirit dries up the bones" (Proverbs 17:22).

The gleamers have learned to cast away their anxieties by praying through the Word and leaving their burdens before the Lord. What's more, they're able to receive his love and share it in turn. Those who delight in the Word love it; they love the One who gave the Word and are also able to love their neighbor.

A wise person is blessed with prosperity. Verse 3 says "Whatever he does, he prospers." A person who meditates on the Word has prosperity in his path. A similar promise is given to Joshua: "This book of the law shall not depart from your mouth, but you shall meditate on it day and night, so that you may be careful to do according to all that is written in it; for then you will make your way prosperous, and then you will have success" (Joshua 1:8).

The biblical notion of prosperity doesn't mean we won't encounter problems. But Scripture teaches that we'll prosper in spite of the problems. A scriptural understanding of prosperity means that we'll accomplish God-ordained tasks. For Joshua, it was conquering the land of Canaan. For Nehemiah, it was rebuilding the wall of Jerusalem. For our Lord Jesus, it was redeeming humanity on the cross.

Those who meditate on the Word will not only prosper, they'll ultimately enjoy life to the full. When Jesus told us, "I came that they may have life, and have it abundantly" (John 10:10), in one sense he was saying it to those who meditate on his Word.

A tree planted by the streams of water will never die of thirst; its leaves are green, and the tree bears much fruit. As such, a person rooted in the Lord Jesus receives an unending supply of living water and will live a full spiritual life.

Isaiah expressed this reality well:

And the LORD will continually guide you,
    And satisfy your desire in scorched places,
    And give strength to your bones;
    And you will be like a watered garden,
    And like a spring of water whose waters do not fail.
    (Isaiah 58:11)

We're called to become "watered gardens"; we're called to share his blessing. But the ultimate goal of prosperity is to bear fruit to share with others.

Psalm 1 tells us who "the blessed person" is. It also tells us how we may become such a person. As we've seen, a blessed person is a wise person; meditating on the Word is the road to becoming such a person.

Therefore, we must be rooted in Jesus Christ, who is the Word. Paul tells us to be "rooted and . . . built up in Him and established in your faith, just as you were instructed, and overflowing with gratitude" (Colossians 2:7). Jesus is the Word. He's the living water. When we become rooted in him, we become like a tree planted by the streams of water and become fruitful: "No longer do I not call you slaves, for the slave does not know what his master is doing; but I have called you friends, for all things that I have heard from My Father I have made known to you" (John 15:15).

A more amazing truth is that when we abide in Jesus, we'll not only bear fruit in season, we can actually bear fruit all the time. Jesus tells us, "You did not choose Me but I chose you, and appointed you that you would go and bear fruit, and that your fruit would remain, so that whatever you ask of the Father in My name He may give to you" (John 15:16).

I pray that you'll be rooted in the Lord Jesus, abide in his Word (John 8:31) and meditate on his Word, to become fruitful and prosperous in life.

EXPLANATION OF THE MEDITATION

I wanted to gain insight from meditating on Psalm 1. As I meditated on it, I regarded the cross-references that came to mind as precious. I marveled at how one verse interwove with another and recorded all verses that had some application to my own life.

All of the Scripture verses in this meditation came from my memory. In some cases I didn't recall the entire verse, but I knew their chapter and verse references, and found them easily.

The Word of God is recorded in such a way that it's not too diffi-

cult to recall. A tree, streams of water, roots, leaves, heat, year of famine, fruit, a well-watered garden—all are concrete images that are easy
to visualize.

Other expressions also came to mind easily: the wicked, the sinner, the scoffer and the righteous are clearly distinguished.

Moreover, the psalmist's language is orderly and coherent; his
contrasts between the wicked and the righteous, the fruit and the
chaff, prosperity and judgment are vivid, easy-to-remember
expressions.

As mentioned on page 116, the psalmist is employing the language
of the sixth sense. In fact, he's using traumatic language to describe
the life of the wicked; he wants it to impact our memory. In the end,
elements that are critical for memorization, such as content, sound,
color and position, create a harmonious whole.

The content of the first psalm is particularly rich for meditation.
It contains the universal desire to be blessed, to prosper and to avoid
judgment. Festooning these are the images of streams flowing, trees
growing, tastes maturing.

Again, I would like to stress the importance of the Word dwelling
in our hearts. The relationship between what we've already committed to memory in the past and the text of meditation at hand will
yield even more insight.

When these connections occur, we experience a sort of symphony
within our mind and a theme of beauty resounds. When this kind of
music occurs, the Lord Jesus becomes the conductor of an incredible
concert; all of the inspired Word centers on him to the glory of the
Father (John 5:39).

Psalm 1 is what we focused on, but it fruitfully connects with the
rest of Scripture in relation to Jesus Christ.

The root of a deepened meditation lies in Scripture memorization, and so does the root of spirituality. A truly inspiring sermon or
essay also depends on Scripture remembered.

The more we commit the Word to memory, the richer our being
becomes. The melodious concert of his Word will continually echo

within us. Then we'll encounter the conductor, our Lord Jesus, the Holy Spirit, who helps us to remember the Scriptures, and the Father, who'll receive glory through all of this.

I pray that learning Scripture by heart will lead you, reader and memorizer, to the blessed life.

Appendix

Favorite Passages for Memorization

Imprinting Scripture on the Heart

Keep these words that I am commanding you today in your heart. (Deuteronomy 6:6)

Keep my commandments and live,
   keep my teachings as the apple of your eye;
bind them on your fingers,
   write them on the tablet of your heart. (Proverbs 7:2-3)

Storing Verses Up in the Heart

Receive instruction from his mouth,
   and lay up his words in your heart. (Job 22:22)

I have not departed from the commandment of his lips;
   I have treasured in my bosom the words of his mouth.
(Job 23:12)

My child, if you accept my words
   and treasure up my commandments within you,
making your ear attentive to wisdom
   and inclining your heart to understanding;
if you indeed cry out for insight,
   and raise your voice for understanding;
if you seek it like silver,
   and search for it as for hidden treasures—

then you will understand the fear of the LORD
and find the knowledge of God. (Proverbs 2:1-5)

MEDITATING ON THE WORD

This book of the law shall not depart out of your mouth; you shall meditate on it day and night, so that you may be careful to act in accordance with all that is written in it. For then you shall make your way prosperous, and then you shall be successful. (Joshua 1:8)

But their delight is in the law of the LORD,
and on his law they meditate day and night.
They are like trees planted by streams of water,
which yield their fruit in its season,
and their leaves do not wither.
In all that they do, they prosper. (Psalm 1:2-3)

EATING THE WORD OF GOD

Your words were found, and I ate them,
and your words became to me a joy
and the delight of my heart;
for I am called by your name,
O LORD, God of hosts. (Jeremiah 15:16)

He said to me, Mortal, eat this scroll that I give you and fill your stomach with it. Then I ate it; and in my mouth it was as sweet as honey. (Ezekiel 3:3)

THE WORD OF GOD AND WISDOM

Your commandment makes me wiser than my enemies,
for it is always with me.
I have more understanding than all my teachers,
for your decrees are my meditation.
I understand more than the aged,
for I keep your precepts. (Psalm 119:98-100)

Let the word of Christ dwell in you richly; teach and admonish one another in all wisdom; and with gratitude in your hearts sing psalms, hymns, and spiritual songs to God. (Colossians 3:16)

THE WORD OF GOD AND SPIRITUAL WARFARE

Take the helmet of salvation, and the sword of the Spirit, which is the word of God. (Ephesians 6:17)

I write to you, children,
   because you know the Father.
I write to you, fathers,
   because you know him who is from the beginning.
I write to you, young people,
   because you are strong
   and the word of God abides in you,
      and you have overcome the evil one. (1 John 2:14)

THE WORD OF GOD AND EDUCATION

Keep these words that I am commanding you today in your heart. Recite them to your children and talk about them when you are at home and when you are away, when you lie down and when you rise. Bind them as a sign on your hand, fix them as an emblem on your forehead, and write them on the doorposts of your house and on your gates. (Deuteronomy 6:6-9)

All scripture is inspired by God and is useful for teaching, for reproof, for correction, and for training in righteousness, so that everyone who belongs to God may be proficient, equipped for every good work. (2 Timothy 3:16-17)

THE WORD OF GOD AND PRACTICING IT

Ezra had set his heart to study the law of the LORD, and to do it, and to teach the statutes and ordinances in Israel. (Ezra 7:10)

Whoever breaks one of the least of these commandments, and teaches others to do the same, will be called least in the kingdom of heaven; but whoever does them and teaches them will be called great in the kingdom of heaven. (Matthew 5:19)

THE WORD OF GOD AND PRAYER

If you abide in me, and my words abide in you, ask for whatever you wish, and it will be done for you. (John 15:7)

In him every one of God's promises is a "Yes." For this reason it is through him that we say the "Amen," to the glory of God. (2 Corinthians 1:20)

THE POWER OF THE WORD OF GOD

Indeed, the word of God is living and active, sharper than any two-edged sword, piercing until it divides soul from spirit, joints from marrow; it is able to judge the thoughts and intentions of the heart. (Hebrews 4:12)

By faith we understand that the worlds were prepared by the word of God, so that what is seen was made from things that are not visible. (Hebrews 11:3)

THE BENEFITS OF THE WORD OF GOD

Every word of God proves true;
    he is a shield to those who take refuge in him.
(Proverbs 30:5)

This is my comfort in my distress,
    that your promise gives me life. (Psalm 119:50)

THE WORD OF GOD AND AFFLICTION IN THE WORLD

Before I was humbled I went astray,
    but now I keep your word. (Psalm 119:67)

It is good for me that I was humbled,
>   so that I might learn your statutes. (Psalms 119:71)

THE GOSPEL CHANGES PEOPLE

For God so loved the world that he gave his only Son, so that everyone who believes in him may not perish but may have eternal life. (John 3:16)

I am not ashamed of the gospel; it is the power of God for salvation to everyone who has faith, to the Jew first and also to the Greek. (Romans 1:16)

THINKING THE GOOD THINGS

Finally, beloved, whatever is true, whatever is honorable, whatever is just, whatever is pure, whatever is pleasing, whatever is commendable, if there is any excellence and if there is anything worthy of praise, think about these things. (Philippians 4:8)

Therefore, holy brothers, who share in the heavenly calling, fix your thoughts on Jesus, the apostle and high priest whom we confess. (Hebrews 3:1 NIV)

THE MEDITATION OF HEART

Let the words of my mouth and the meditation of my heart
>   be acceptable to you,
>   O LORD, my rock and my redeemer. (Psalm 19:14)

I commune with my heart in the night;
>   I meditate and search my spirit. (Psalm 77:6)

GUARDING THE HEART

Keep your heart with all vigilance,
>   for from it flow the springs of life. (Proverbs 4:23)

Do not worry about anything, but in everything by prayer and supplication with thanksgiving let your requests be made known to God. And the peace of God, which surpasses all understanding, will guard your hearts and your minds in Christ Jesus. (Philippians 4:6-7)

STRENGTHENING INNER BEING

I pray that, according to the riches of his glory, he may grant that you may be strengthened in your inner being with power through his Spirit. (Ephesians 3:16)

Be strong in the Lord and in the strength of his power. (Ephesians 6:10)

RENEWING OF THE INNER WORLD

Do not be conformed to this world, but be transformed by the renewing of your minds, so that you may discern what is the will of God—what is good and acceptable and perfect. (Romans 12:2)

So we do not lose heart. Even though our outer nature is wasting away, our inner nature is being renewed day by day. (2 Corinthians 4:16)

CULTIVATING OF THE INNER BEING

Do not adorn yourselves outwardly by braiding your hair, and by wearing gold ornaments or fine clothing; rather, let your adornment be the inner self with the lasting beauty of a gentle and quiet spirit, which is very precious in God's sight. (1 Peter 3:3-4)

My little children, . . . I am again in the pain of childbirth until Christ is formed in you. (Galatians 4:19)

DISCIPLESHIP AND THE LIFE OF BEARING FRUIT

My Father is glorified by this, that you bear much fruit and become my disciples. (John 15:8)

The fruit of the Spirit is love, joy, peace, patience, kindness, generosity, faithfulness, gentleness, and self-control. There is no law against such things. (Galatians 5:22-23)

GROWING IN THE KNOWLEDGE OF GOD

So that you may lead lives worthy of the Lord, fully pleasing to him, as you bear fruit in every good work and as you grow in the knowledge of God. (Colossians 1:10)

Grow in the grace and knowledge of our Lord and Savior Jesus Christ. To him be the glory both now and to the day of eternity. Amen. (2 Peter 3:18)

THE DEEPER LIFE

Deep calls to deep
    at the thunder of your cataracts;
all your waves and your billows
    have gone over me.
(Psalms 42:7)

These things God has revealed to us through the Spirit; for the Spirit searches everything, even the depths of God.
(1 Corinthians 2:10)

DEEP-ROOTED IN CHRIST

As you therefore have received Christ Jesus the Lord, continue to live your lives in him, rooted and built up in him and established in the faith, just as you were taught, abounding in thanksgiving. (Colossians 2:6-7)

That Christ may dwell in your hearts through faith, as you are being rooted and grounded in love. (Ephesians 3:17)

SOLITUDE

In the morning, while it was still very dark, he got up and went out to a deserted place, and there he prayed. (Mark 1:35)

When Jesus realized that they were about to come and take him by force to make him king, he withdrew again to the mountain by himself. (John 6:15)

STILLNESS

Be still, and know that I am God!
    I am exalted among the nations,
    I am exalted in the earth. (Psalm 46:10)

Thus said the Lord GOD, the Holy One of Israel:
In returning and rest you shall be saved;
    in quietness and in trust shall be your strength.
    But you refused. (Isaiah 30:15)

KNOWING GOD

Let us press on to know the LORD;
    his appearing is as sure as the dawn;
he will come to us like the showers,
    like the spring rains that water the earth. (Hosea 6:3)

This is eternal life, that they may know you, the only true God, and Jesus Christ whom you have sent. (John 17:3)

TRUSTING IN GOD

Commit your way to the LORD;
    trust in him, and he will act. (Psalm 37:5)

Blessed are those who trust in the LORD,
    whose trust is the LORD.
They shall be like a tree planted by water,
    sending out its roots by the stream.

It shall not fear when heat comes,
   and its leaves shall stay green;
in the year of drought it is not anxious,
and it does not cease to bear fruit. (Jeremiah 17:7-8)

WAITING FOR GOD

Wait for the LORD;
   be strong, and let your heart take courage;
wait for the LORD! (Psalm 27:14)

I wait for the LORD, my soul waits,
   and in his word I hope;
my soul waits for the Lord
   more than those who watch for the morning,
   more than those who watch for the morning.
(Psalm 130:5-6)

DESIRING GOD

As a deer longs for flowing streams,
   so my soul longs for you, O God. (Psalm 42:1)

O God, you are my God, I seek you,
   my soul thirsts for you;
my flesh faints for you,
   as in a dry and weary land where there is no water.
(Psalm 63:1)

WORSHIPING GOD

The hour is coming, and is now here, when the true worshipers
will worship the Father in spirit and truth, for the Father seeks
such as these to worship him. God is spirit, and those who worship him must worship in spirit and truth. (John 4:23-24)

The twenty-four elders fall before the one who is seated on the
throne and worship the one who lives forever and ever; they cast

their crowns before the throne, singing,
"You are worthy, our Lord and God,
to receive glory and honor and power,
for you created all things,
and by your will they existed and were created."
(Revelation 4:10-11)

THE FEAR OF THE LORD

The fear of the LORD is the beginning of wisdom,
and the knowledge of the Holy One is insight.
(Proverbs 9:10)

He will be the stability of your times,
abundance of salvation, wisdom, and knowledge;
the fear of the LORD is Zion's treasure. (Isaiah 33:6)

GAZING ON THE LORD

One thing I asked of the LORD,
that will I seek after:
to live in the house of the LORD
all the days of my life,
to behold the beauty of the LORD,
and to inquire in his temple. (Psalm 27:4)

And all of us, with unveiled faces, seeing the glory of the Lord
as though reflected in a mirror, are being transformed into the
same image from one degree of glory to another; for this comes
from the Lord, the Spirit. (2 Corinthians 3:18)

THE COMFORT OF GOD

Blessed are those who mourn, for they will be comforted.
(Matthew 5:4)

Blessed be the God and Father of our Lord Jesus Christ, the Father
of mercies and the God of all consolation. (2 Corinthians 1:3)

FELLOWSHIP WITH GOD

God is faithful; by him you were called into the fellowship of his Son, Jesus Christ our Lord. (1 Corinthians 1:9)

We declare to you what we have seen and heard so that you also may have fellowship with us; and truly our fellowship is with the Father and with his Son Jesus Christ. (1 John 1:3)

ANOINTING

God anointed Jesus of Nazareth with the Holy Spirit and with power; . . . he went about doing good and healing all who were oppressed by the devil, for God was with him. (Acts 10:38)

As for you, the anointing that you received from him abides in you, and so you do not need anyone to teach you. But as his anointing teaches you about all things, and is true and is not a lie, and just as it has taught you, abide in him. (1 John 2:27)

HEARING GOD

Samuel said,
"Has the LORD as great delight in burnt offerings and
        sacrifices,
    as in obeying the voice of the LORD?
Surely, to obey is better than sacrifice,
    and to heed than the fat of rams." (1 Samuel 15:22)

Why do you spend your money for that which is not bread,
    and your labor for that which does not satisfy?
Listen carefully to me, and eat what is good,
    and delight yourselves in rich food.
Incline your ear, and come to me;
    listen, so that you may live.
I will make with you an everlasting covenant,
    my steadfast, sure love for David. (Isaiah 55:2-3)

Obedience

They who have my commandments and keep them are those who love me; and those who love me will be loved by my Father, and I will love them and reveal myself to them. (John 14:21)

Just as by the one man's disobedience the many were made sinners, so by the one man's obedience the many will be made righteous. (Romans 5:19)

Joy

Rejoice always, pray without ceasing, give thanks in all circumstances; for this is the will of God in Christ Jesus for you. (1 Thessalonians 5:16-18)

Although you have not seen him, you love him; and even though you do not see him now, you believe in him and rejoice with an indescribable and glorious joy, for you are receiving the outcome of your faith, the salvation of your souls. (1 Peter 1:8-9)

Thanksgiving

Those who bring thanksgiving as their sacrifice honor me;
    to those who go the right way
    I will show the salvation of God. (Psalm 50:23)

Whatever you do, in word or deed, do everything in the name of the Lord Jesus, giving thanks to God the Father through him. (Colossians 3:17)

Patience

Be patient, therefore, beloved, until the coming of the Lord. The farmer waits for the precious crop from the earth, being patient with it until it receives the early and the late rains. (James 5:7)

"I will surely bless you and multiply you." And thus Abraham, having patiently endured, obtained the promise. (Hebrews 6:14-15)

PERSEVERANCE

My brothers and sisters, whenever you face trials of any kind, consider it nothing but joy, because you know that the testing of your faith produces endurance; and let endurance have its full effect, so that you may be mature and complete, lacking in nothing. (James 1:2-4)

Indeed we call blessed those who showed endurance. You have heard of the endurance of Job, and you have seen the purpose of the Lord, how the Lord is compassionate and merciful. (James 5:11)

LOVE

Beloved, since God loved us so much, we also ought to love one another. (1 John 4:11)

There is no fear in love, but perfect love casts out fear; for fear has to do with punishment, and whoever fears has not reached perfection in love. (1 John 4:18)

GODLINESS

Have nothing to do with profane myths and old wives' tales. Train yourself in godliness, for, while physical training is of some value, godliness is valuable in every way, holding promise for both the present life and the life to come. (1 Timothy 4:7-8)

For this very reason, you must make every effort to support your faith with goodness, and goodness with knowledge, and knowledge with self-control, and self-control with endurance, and endurance with godliness, and godliness with mutual affection, and mutual affection with love. (2 Peter 1:5-7)

FAITHFULNESS

His master said to him, "Well done, good and trustworthy slave; you have been trustworthy in a few things, I will put you in charge of many things; enter into the joy of your master." (Matthew 25:21)

Christ, however, was faithful over God's house as a son, and we are his house if we hold firm the confidence and the pride that belong to hope. (Hebrews 3:6)

HUMILITY

He humbled himself
and became obedient to the point of death—
even death on a cross. (Philippians 2:8)

Humble yourselves therefore under the mighty hand of God, so that he may exalt you in due time. (1 Peter 5:6)

GENTLENESS

But the meek shall inherit the land,
and delight themselves in abundant prosperity.
(Psalm 37:11)

Take my yoke upon you, and learn from me; for I am gentle and humble in heart, and you will find rest for your souls. (Matthew 11:29)

COURAGE

I hereby command you: Be strong and courageous; do not be frightened or dismayed, for the LORD your God is with you wherever you go. (Joshua 1:9)

Be strong, and let your heart take courage,
all you who wait for the LORD. (Psalms 31:24)

PEACE

Those of steadfast mind you keep in peace—
in peace because they trust in you. (Isaiah 26:3)

Let the peace of Christ rule in your hearts, to which indeed you were called in the one body. And be thankful. (Colossians 3:15)

FORGIVENESS

If you forgive others their trespasses, your heavenly Father will also forgive you. (Matthew 6:14)

Be kind to one another, tenderhearted, forgiving one another, as God in Christ has forgiven you. (Ephesians 4:32)

LOVING OUR ENEMY

You have heard that it was said, "You shall love your neighbor and hate your enemy." But I say to you, Love your enemies and pray for those who persecute you. (Matthew 5:43-44)

Beloved, never avenge yourselves, but leave room for the wrath of God; for it is written, "Vengeance is mine, I will repay, says the Lord." No, "if your enemies are hungry, feed them; if they are thirsty, give them something to drink; for by doing this you will heap burning coals on their heads." (Romans 12:19-20)

Acknowledgments

This book was birthed in the midst of tough times. There were many spiritual attacks both on the writing process and on me personally as I wrote this book. I guess it was because abiding in the Word of God through memorizing Scripture is what our Lord is most pleased with. For the same reason, Satan hates it. I learned that that was why it was so difficult for me to finish this book. However, the Word of God is so powerful that it enabled me to complete it. So I am also indebted to many people for their prayer support to see this book published.

I'm grateful for the wonderful translation work by Pastors Michael Choi, Byoungchul Joseph Jun (B. J.) and Doug Spriggs. I cannot thank Emilie Griffin and William Griffin enough for their helpful feedback and support for this project. Their editing work was full of love and passion. I also thank Cindy Bunch for her constant encouragement, which contributed greatly to the publishing of this book.

Special thanks to Dr. Dallas Willard for writing the foreword. It was through his books that I learned how important Scripture memorization is for our spiritual formation and growth. Many thanks go out to Richard J. Foster. His writings guided and led me deeper spiritually. Without his support and encouragement, this book could not have come about.

I also thank my mother, who has prayed for me through her entire life, and I thank my wife, Grace, and my precious two daughters, Rebekah and Esther, for their love and prayer support. My special recognition also goes to our new family members, Daniel, my son-in-law, and our first grandchild, Jillian.

Finally, I want to give my utmost thanks to Jesus who overcame Satan's temptations by using the Scriptures that he memorized himself. I am so very grateful that Jesus completed his work of salvation on the cross by memorizing Scripture.